# THE WAY
# WE LIVED THEN
## BUNGAY IN THE 1930's

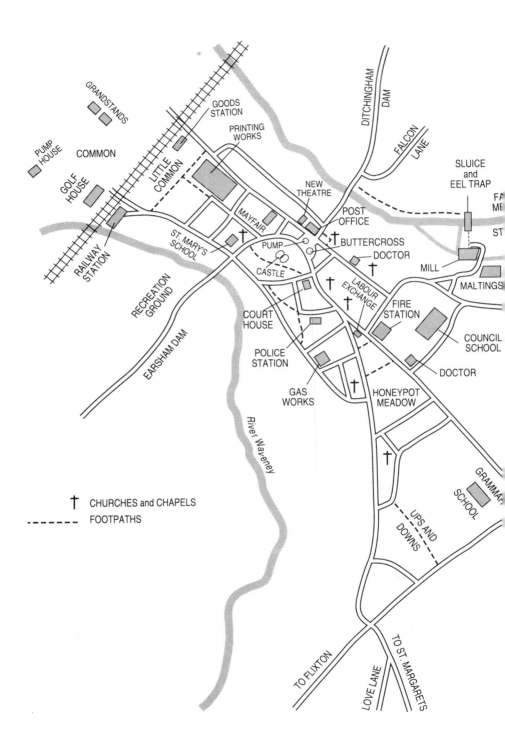

GRANDSTANDS

PUMP HOUSE

COMMON

GOLF HOUSE

GOODS STATION

PRINTING WORKS

LITTLE COMMON

DITCHINGHAM DAM

FALCON LANE

NEW THEATRE

SLUICE and EEL TRAP

FA
ME

POST OFFICE

ST

MAYFAIR

† BUTTERCROSS

RAILWAY STATION

ST. MARY'S SCHOOL

PUMP

† DOCTOR

MILL

CASTLE

MALTINGS

RECREATION GROUND

LABOUR EXCHANGE

FIRE STATION

EARSHAM DAM

COURT HOUSE

COUNCIL SCHOOL

POLICE STATION

DOCTOR

GAS WORKS

HONEYPOT MEADOW

†

River Waveney

†

GRAMMAR SCHOOL

† CHURCHES and CHAPELS

- - - - - FOOTPATHS

UPS AND DOWNS

TO FLIXTON

LOVE LANE

TO ST. MARGARETS

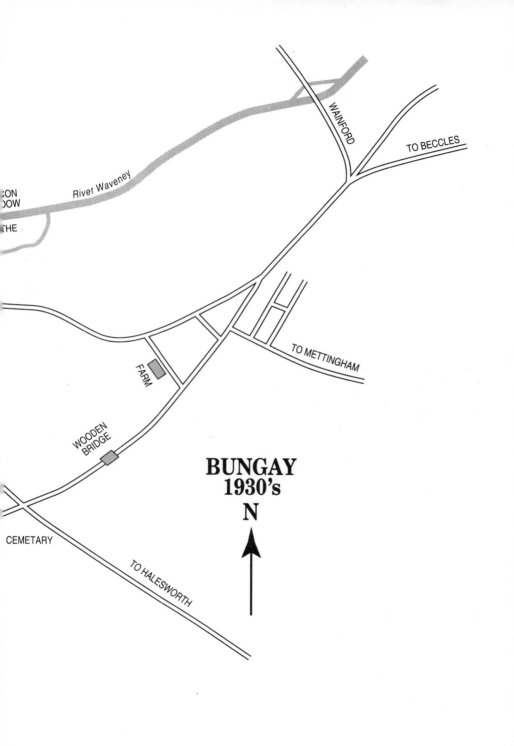

This book is dedicated to all my friends and acquaintances who did not live to see the consequences of the changes that took place in this decade.

STAITHE ROAD

Illustrations kindly supplied by Frank Honeywood, Town Recorder.

# THE WAY
# WE LIVED THEN
## BUNGAY IN THE 1930's

BY
MALCOLM BEDINGFIELD

MORROW & CO
PUBLISHERS
BUNGAY SUFFOLK
1994

Published by MORROW & CO. Publishers Bungay Suffolk.
1994.

British Library cataloguing in Publications Data

ISBN 0 948903 18 X

Reproduction and maps - © NIDGE PRINTGRAPHICS BUNGAY

Printed by the Ipswich Book Company

# CONTENTS.

Maps.

Foreword.

Introduction.                           Page.   1.
   1. A General View.              "       5.
   2. Work and Prospects.          "      15.
   3. The People.                  "      21.
   4. Transport.                   "      40.
   5. Services.                    "      54.
   6. Children - At School.        "      63.
   7. Children - At Leisure.       "      75.
   8. The Shops and Workers.       "      91.
   9. Law and Order.               "     108.
10. The River and the Common.           "     119.
11. Pastimes and Leisure.               "     135.
12. Events Through the Year.            "     147.
13. Health and Welfare.                 "     166.
14. A Summary.                          "     174.

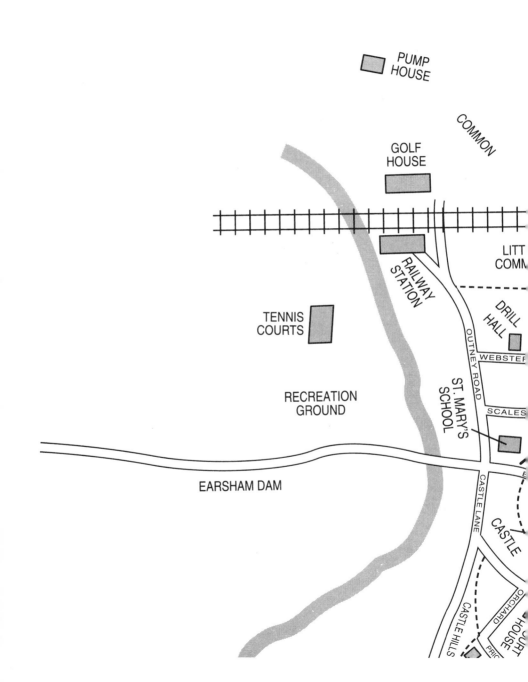

PUMP
HOUSE

COMMON

GOLF
HOUSE

LITT
COMM

RAILWAY
STATION

DRILL
HALL

WEBSTER

OUTNEY ROAD

TENNIS
COURTS

ST. MARY'S
SCHOOL

SCALES

RECREATION
GROUND

EARSHAM DAM

CASTLE LANE

CASTLE

ORCHARD

COURT
HOUSE

PRIC

CASTLE HILLS

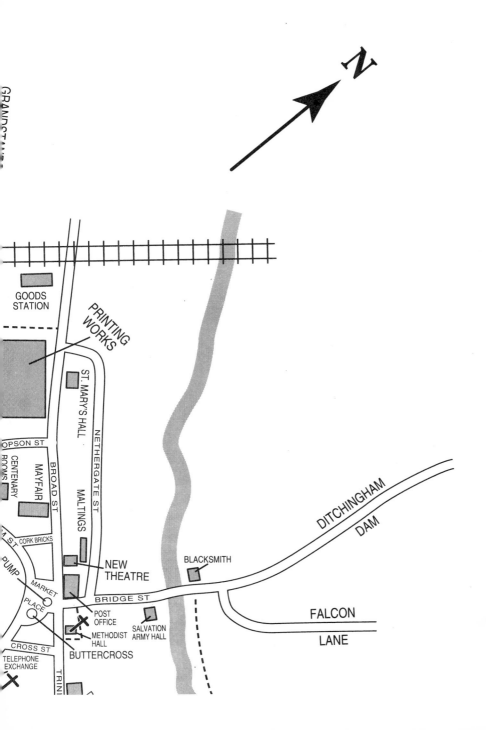

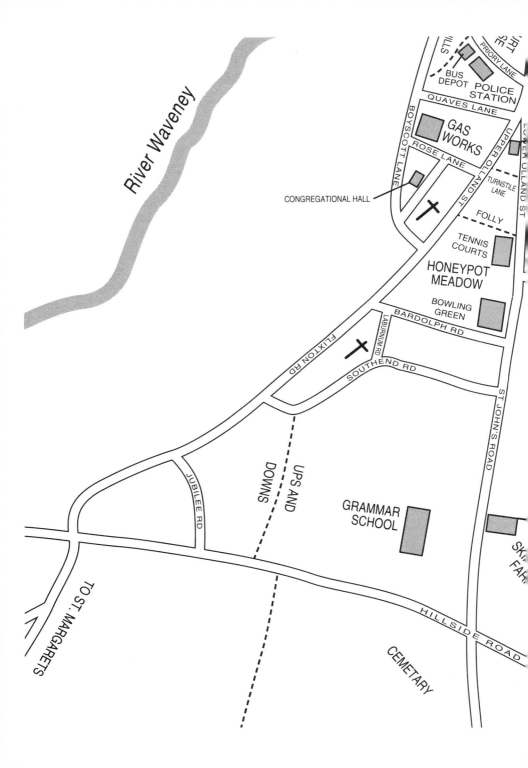

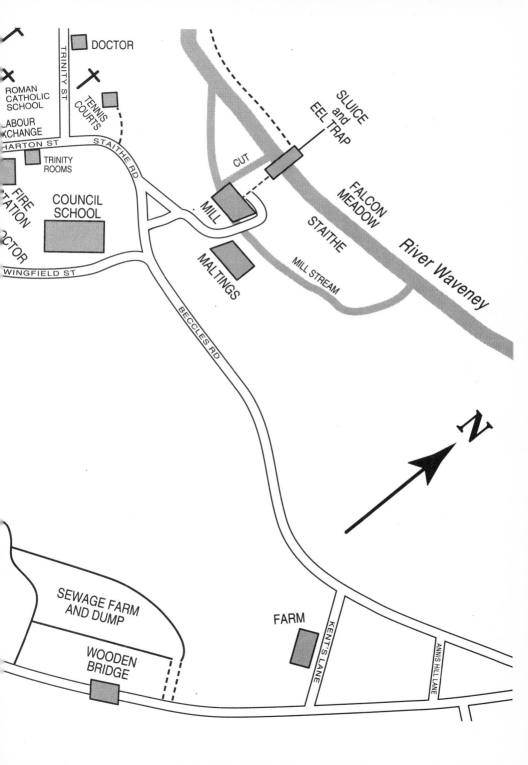

# FOREWORD.

Do you remember? must be one of the most frequent questions elderly folk ask one another when they meet and start up a conversation and it is invariably the good and happy times which are discussed. As stories and incidents are related, others, which were forgotten long ago, spring to mind. I find it sad to think in a few years time there will be no one to remember and reminisce about the days of my childhood which, like many of my generation, I enjoy discussing and comparing with people's expectations today. To make the most of the time left I have written about life and conditions during the years I was growing up exactly as I remember them in the hope that this book will give pleasure to those of the same age group by stirring happy memories of their own as well as giving others the opportunity to compare today's society with one that has long since passed. I hope that whoever reads this will experience at least some of the immense pleasure I got writing it.

# THE WAY WE LIVED THEN
# BUNGAY IN THE 1930's.

# INTRODUCTION.

Progress has always been dependant on communication and in a small market town in the early 1930's information was only available to the ordinary people through the newspapers, posters, the Royal Mail or by word of mouth. Telegrams were reserved for emergencies and the telephone for larger businesses or the rich. Only the better off were able to afford wireless which was just emerging from accumulator powered sets with headphones to mass produced radios run from a main electric supply. As yet there were very few working class households with electricity or water mains connected.

Rail and bus were the main means of transport and generally these served the inhabitants quite well although people did not travel far from their town or village and really had little cause to do so as all their everyday needs were available from the local stores. The villagers highlight of the week was a trip into town on Saturday night which cost a few pence on the bus or train, unless they used their bicycle. There they would buy that something special they were unable to get at their local shop or perhaps

1

have a hair cut or a few drinks at the public house of their choice with friends and acquaintances and listen to the news and stories from other areas. Some would go to the local cinema and many would want to complete the evening out with a fish and chip supper. Bought wrapped in newspaper and generously sprinkled with salt and vinegar, they ate them with their fingers as they walked down the road on their way home.

Life was lived at a leisurely pace with people in small communities largely responsible for themselves. Most accepted the life they had and made every effort to enjoy it and even though times were very hard for many, a strong feeling of fellowship existed within the classes. There were three distinct classes which were very evident in all walks of life in both towns and villages and consisted of the upper [the wealthy], the middle [the business people and shopkeepers] and the working class. This was clearly seen and acknowledged on the railway where carriages were all clearly marked 1st, 2nd or 3rd class in gold coloured paint on the outside of the door of each compartment whose comfort and convenience was in keeping with the occupants social standing.

There were always opportunities for those bright and ambitious youngsters from all of these classes who were prepared to leave home, an action which often meant moving into lodgings in a completely different environment among people they did not know and who had no idea at all what life outside a large town or city was like. There were of course those individuals in every small town and village who had been in the armed forces, particularly during the Great War, always ready to relate their experiences in other parts of the world as well as the British Isles and these stories were often responsible for sowing the first seeds of discontent in young people's minds.

People had little spare time as long hours were worked for quite low pay and their pleasures were simple which is why eager enthusiasm was easily aroused for special events such as fairs, the circus and local sports. Parents had little chance of going to the seaside or having a day out of the town as a family as many had barely enough money each week for food and clothes and keep a roof over their heads. However, there were always outings and parties being arranged by various bodies for the children, while the adults would indulge in their weekly whist drives and socials and give support to local organisations which played an important part in the life of any community no matter how large or small it might be.

By the end of the decade more progress had been made than in any before it and this was mainly due to the improved communications as electricity spread into the homes of ordinary people, raising their expectations and giving them access to many modern facilities at the same time as motorisation replaced the horse. Everyone was influenced by the wireless and the glamour of the cinema and the progress which had so far advanced steadily accelerated as life took on a new urgency in the last two or three years when the threat of war became a reality. Suddenly, things like class distinction became unimportant as bosses and workers and rich and poor all worked together to do whatever was asked of them as the country strove desperately to build up it's defences.

The town I grew up in was typical of many small market towns to be found all over the country and the historical facts have already been detailed by others in earlier publications. This book relates specifically to the 1930's and in the pages which follow I will write the facts and detail the situations as I remember them in the hope that I am able to give the reader an insight into the lives of people at the time of my childhood and some idea of their aspirations and problems as well as a general feeling of what it would have been like to have lived at that time. It must be borne in mind that my memory and perception is through the eyes of a young boy whose childhood could not have been comparable with all other children of the same age and who's views must have been very different to those of an adult.

FIRE BRIGADE WITH TENDER

DELIVERING MILK IN CHAUCER STREET

# CHAPTER 1.

## A GENERAL VIEW.

Situated in a loop of the river Waveney, Bungay had been an important town for many years serving the surrounding villages as well as some 3,000 inhabitants.The elected Urban District Council with fifteen members was mostly made up of business men with quite heavy responsibilities including such things as the upkeep of the roads, water supply, drains and sewerage, street lighting [some of which was still gas] and the general welfare of the residents. One of the major priorities of the council had always been, and still was, to retain as much of it's independence as possible. The town had it's own water supply pumped from under the Common which was reputed to be inexhaustible and well able to meet the growing demand as it was piped directly into more and more households. It also had it's own gas works and electric company which was privately owned and bought in power from the Great Yarmouth power station. Volunteers manned the fire engine at the fire station in Cross Street which, at the beginning of the decade, was still horse drawn. This meant the horses would have to be fetched from the Common before they could answer a call but this soon changed with the building of the new fire station in Lower Olland Street and the purchase of a motorised engine.

A very old town, Bungay is able to boast of the ruins which were once Bigod's Castle and it was during this period that Dr. L. B. Cane started to raise enthusiasm and then the money to preserve the remains. The publicity it was given started many tales of tunnels and passages which supposedly ran in all directions, one of them far enough to make a connection with Mettingham Castle which would have made that particular tunnel almost two miles long. Such stories had to include various encounters with ghosts and more than one person laid claim to have experienced strange sightings and happenings.

Shops and businesses were plentiful and varied and catered for every need. The population seemed to be split into areas, each of them having easily accessible suppliers. Bridge Street had shops on both sides from the Market Place down to the bridge which included a baker, grocer, greengrocer, dairy, confectioner, wet and fried fish shops, barber, watchmaker, saddler and just over the bridge a blacksmith. These served their locals with their immediate needs while the residents around Boyscott Lane, where the gasworks was situated, were well catered for by the tradesmen in Upper Olland Street. The population living at the Back of the Hills and Trinity Street had easy access to the main shopping areas of St Mary's Street and Earsham Street. Generally people would purchase their needs daily as required. In fact those that bought their milk from the dairy would most likely take their jug or milk can morning and evening to have the required amount measured out of a large urn thus ensuring it to be fresh from the last milking. Besides the dairies and surrounding dairy farmers, there was a milking parlour in Broad Street as well as one in Flixton Road and a smallholding in Wharton Street where milk and cream could be bought immediately after milking.

Food was always bought fresh unless it was dried or tinned and most greengrocery was locally grown so except for those things that were available in tins or preserved, all fruit and vegetables were seasonal. This not only ensured a changed basic menu through the year but created friendly competition between householders who had a garden or allotment to see who would be soonest taking up new potatoes or gathering the earliest mess of peas and for others to see which shop could be the first to get supplies as produce came into season. Butchers had a cold safe to keep their meat in which was no more than a small wooden room with ice packed in the walls and was dependant on the ice man making his delivery of ice blocks twice a week. During opening hours and particularly at times like Christmas, sides of pork, beef and mutton as well as poultry would be hung outside the shops for all to see. Livestock was killed on the premises usually twice a week so even during a hot spell in summer meat would always be quite fresh.

There was very little motorised transport as yet so all local deliveries were made by horse and cart or handcart. Supplies for the shops, milk deliveries to other towns and villages, things like fish from the coastal ports and livestock were transported by the railway. Roads in the town were not too congested and they were wide enough for two wagons to pass. The largest of these to be seen regularly would be the coal cart and the wagon pulled by a pair of Shires which came up from the mill at the Staithe every weekday to make deliveries to local warehouses or farms. At sometime of the day on every street or road you could expect to see a milkman in a horse drawn cart, a baker's roundsman pulling a purpose built handcart full of bread, an oilman selling paraffin and hardware from his cart as well as many other tradesmen plying their goods around the town and villages. On the main roads only the occasional bus, lorry or motor cycle would be encountered and in the mornings and evenings when people were going to and from work a few bicycles would be on the roads but mostly everyone walked. When the schools were closed there were always children to be found playing their favourite games on the pavements and mingling among the other road users with their hoops and tops but at haymaking or harvest time when the really big wagons came through the town they, like everyone else, had to get out of the way.

Some of the more modern houses had flush toilets, generally built on outside the main building, with an inside tap over a shallow sink in the kitchen but many still depended on a pump for their water. This was complimented by a water butt or cistern which collected all the water from the roof and was sometimes built of bricks and joined onto the back of the house. This water would be used when the copper fire was lit, usually on Monday and Friday or Saturday, for the weekly wash and for the family to bath. When the weather permitted the washing was often done in a tin bath on a wooden bench or stool outside the back door. Other times it had to be done in a very small steam filled kitchen.

Cooking for the more fortunate families was done was over a cooking range but for others it was on the hob over the fire or in an oven in the wall for which another fire had to be lit. Some houses therefore had as many as three fireplaces in the kitchen, one for pots and pans, one for the copper and another for the oven. Bearing in mind the standard of living endured by most people it is unlikely many had one burning for very long. One alternative was to have an oil stove and an oil oven which was probably much cheaper and more convenient once you had paid for them, so most of the people who could afford to bought them, unless of course they had gas which was better still.

Electricity was being installed in new houses but it was a luxury very few could afford to enjoy. The larger old dwellings had gas which gave them another alternative method of cooking. Gas was also still used for the street lighting and it was a familiar sight at dusk to see the lamplighter with his pole going about his business. Households generally used paraffin lamps for lighting while everyone had a candle in a candlestick to light the way up the stairs to bed. The local electric light company was at this time offering to put a single light with an enamel shade in four rooms at a cost of twenty-five shillings and anyone who accepted the offer could have an extra one put anywhere free of charge. A single two-pin socket would be about five shillings more and this was a major step toward the luxury of constant hot water because anyone with an electric socket could now have an electric kettle. Unfortunately, however cheap this all seemed it was a long way out of reach for a great many people.

The middle and upper classes were beginning to indulge and enjoy the progress which was evident to if not achievable by everyone. There were one or two owners of motor cars and motorcycles in the town and one tradesman, a grocer in Upper Olland Street, did his deliveries in a bright red van with OXO painted in large letters on both sides. There was no fear of it getting a puncture on the rough uneven roads as the tyres were made of solid rubber. The next to be motorised was probably the baker in St. Mary's Street who had his bread cart fitted on to the front of a motorcycle. It seemed to work very well. Others followed through the 1930's and It was a sad day when the Shire horses pulling the wagon from the mill at the Staithe were replaced by, what seemed at the time, a big ugly lorry.

Every household had their regular callers, the daily tradesmen, the oilman, greengrocer and people calling once or twice a week. Then there were those that came round any time like door to door salesmen, gypsies who always seemed to come back and the occasional tramp asking for hot water for his tea who was quite willing to accept anything else that might be offered him. Very few women worked other than in the home looking after their families and that was a full time job. Their houses were terraced or built very close together which meant there was always someone near at hand so they were not likely to be lonely or frightened by anything when their menfolk were away. The working class had little or no fear of burglars or such, they didn't have very much worth stealing but more important, anyone with the idea would be aware of the chance of being seen and recognised in a place where everyone knows everyone else. Neighbours were generally very friendly toward one another and would always find time to chat and pass on any news or discuss their problems. The tradesmen and people calling at the door were a good source of information as they went from house to house and anything of interest would be passed on between husband and wife in the evening, for with no radio or television and the room lit only by oil lamp and firelight on dark winter nights people needed to be able to converse. Although there were newspapers and books, reading under such conditions was a strain.

Bungay was a thriving town and something was always going on. Tuesday and Thursday were market days when stalls would be laid out under the Butter Cross and livestock would be auctioned at the sale ground which was situated on the castle grounds behind the White Lion public house in Earsham Street. These were busy days for the town when people would come in from the other nearby towns and villages to sell their wares and replenish their stocks. There were frequent visits by touring circuses and fairs who would advertise on all available billboards, in local shops and anywhere they thought a poster would be seen. During the better weather hardly a week would pass without a fete or sports of some kind in aid of one of the local organisations. The town's football team played it's fixtures on the Recreation Ground on Earsham Dam having moved from the Honeypot Meadow a few years before and still received good support. Other sporting activities were evident with the bowls club in Lower Olland Street, tennis courts on the Honeypot Meadow, the Recreation Ground and the Grammar School Meadow in Staithe Road. The town's cricket team also had it's successes and the golf club ideally situated on the common continued to expand both it's course and membership.

With the river Waveney flowing north and south of the town as well as round the Common, covering a distance of two to three miles, fishing was a popular pastime for both young and old. The usual youth clubs were open in the town for youngsters and membership of the scouts and girl guides was quite strong. There were lots more organisations for children to join and many clubs and societies like the British Legion, Horticultural Society etc. as well as sports clubs for the older generations who had the time and inclination to support them. During the school Summer holidays there was always the Sunday school outing and the day out to the seaside organised by the Oddfellows for the children to look forward to and save those odd pennies for.

The cinema was another great source of pleasure for everyone. The New Theatre, situated in Broad Street, had been built as a playhouse and was still the venue for the odd show but above all it showed films. Talking pictures had just come to Bungay and everyone enjoyed the escapism offered by the glamour of Hollywood. It didn't seem to matter that films were usually years old before they were shown in the smaller towns in the country. Everyone went to the cinema at some time and films and the stars soon became part of everyday conversation. Not only did they provide an important diversion from the hardships people had to endure but they inspired hope and created dreams which in many cases gave the incentive for them to struggle harder to achieve their ambitions. Through the decade their influence on both young and old increased.

Religion played a big part in many peoples lives and the town catered well for a number of different beliefs. St Mary's Church the most prominent place of worship situated in the centre of the town was very well attended at all times and it was not unusual for almost every seat to be filled on special occasions, in fact on Armistice Day the congregation often spilled over into the church grounds. Other churches and chapels were equally well supported. There was the Holy Trinity Church in Trinity Street, the Roman Catholic Church in St. Mary's Street, the Congregational Chapel in Upper Olland Street, the  Methodist Chapel in Trinity Street, the Baptist Chapel in Chaucer Street and the Salvation Army Hall in Bridge Street.

The clock on the tower of St Mary's Church chimed every quarter hour and depending on the direction of the wind, could be heard all over the town. Sunday mornings the church bells would be rung with much enthusiasm for half an hour before the morning service. On one or two evenings during the week the silence, which was usually broken only by the sound of a train entering or leaving the station, would be shattered by the pealing of the bells when the bellringers had their practice. Not so noisy was the Salvation Army band which would play for a time in the Market Place while members passed the plate around among the onlookers and people passing by. They would then progress, playing and singing, down the main streets and roads doing a door to door collection. The other religious organisations had their own methods of collecting money to supplement the collections taken at each service. The appointed committees would organise fetes, jumble sales, whist drives, talks and lectures by prominent citizens, social events etc.. New ideas for raising money were always being sought.

All of the churches and chapels had sunday schools for the young people who were welcome to attend from the age of five to fourteen when those with the necessary aptitude would be encouraged to become teachers. All seniors attending the sunday schools and even some who didn't could join the bible classes in order to be confirmed. The churches all had choir's who had no trouble maintaining a full compliment and were very much appreciated by the congregations especially at the festive services when they could render appropriate anthems and carols, led by their most popular soloists which they would have spent months rehearsing in the evenings. The venue for many of the committee's activities were the church halls. St Mary's was situated in Broad Street and Trinity in Wharton Street while the others were adjoining or adjacent to their place of worship. All of these halls were frequently hired out to local organisations for varies functions.

As a market town Bungay had it's fair share of public houses and inns. Almost every road could boast it's own pub or ale house and there were at least half a dozen of these houses in St Mary's Street and Earsham Street where a traveller or visitor could get refreshment. On market days they all had extended hours and it was not an unusual sight to see someone who had over indulged, perhaps having had a successful day at the market or for reasons of his own, staggering down the street. Even though times were hard the pubs were well patronised. In the evenings men would meet to relate the days events and pass on any bits of gossip they might have heard. The contribution to this from railway staff, bus drivers and anyone whose work took them out of the town was invaluable.

The pubs and the barbers shop were probably the centre of the town's communication where news and views were exchanged. At lunchtime many of the tradespeople would meet and discuss their own varied matters of interest. Besides drinking and talking many relaxed with a game of dominoes, cards, darts, shove halfpenny or a game peculiar to that particular pub. Some offered accommodation at all times but the highlight for all must have been the twice a year when the National Hunt race meetings took place on the Common. Horses, stable boys and other staff would arrive days and sometimes weeks before the actual race days and would be accommodated in every available public house, inn or stable as near to the Common as they could get. There was always great excitement throughout the town at this time as everyone was affected in some way and where better to get first hand news of what was going on than in the local pub. The King's Head hotel in the Market Place also enjoyed the privilege of serving the Stirrup Cup to the local hunt which was very active and could often be seen in full flight by people walking or working in the surrounding countryside.

Accommodation for the working classes was bad. Houses were small and tightly packed in small areas. Many were terraced with one room and a kitchen down and one large bedroom and a small box room upstairs. People brought up quite big families in such places, sometimes as many as six or seven children, with four or five sleeping in the same bed lying alternately head to toe. In the short term this could have been great  fun but being obliged to live under such conditions, bearing in mind the lack of facilities like dependence on a communal tap or pump for water and having to heat it over a fire or oil stove must have created a lot of tension and made even the basic things in life very difficult for both the parents and children.

From the age of five children went to an infants school and even in the villages there was usually a school within walking distance which was sometimes the only one a child would attend, staying there under the same teachers until they reached the age of fourteen. In the town there was a choice if you were a Roman Catholic or if as a middle class citizen you were able to afford to pay the fees of a private school. At the council school in Wingfield Street boys and girls were originally in separate classes, boys going in one end of the building and girls the other, later they became mixed. All pupils reaching the age of ten or eleven took the scholarship exam and a pass entitled them to apply to go to a grammar school. While this would be a great achievement for the child and the parents could be very pleased for them, for many it probably meant extra hardship. There would be a small grant to help pay for the school uniform etc. but it would never be nearly enough to meet all the costs incurred. The parents had many things to consider not least of all the other members of the family, what will happen when it is their turn? Where will the child go to find a quiet corner to do homework? How will they get to school? It might well mean a bus or perhaps a cycle ride. Some pupils attending Bungay Grammar School used both of these methods and the train. Another important fact to consider was the child would now be staying on at school until the age of sixteen to take the School Certificate instead of looking for work to start earning at fourteen. If this applied to the eldest of a large family the biggest financial strain would come just at a time when demand from the rest of the family was on the increase. Bungay Grammar School had 5% of their compliment made up of scholarship pupils with the remainder all paying. A small percentage were boarders staying at two boarding houses, Dunelm in Lower Olland Street and Emmanuel House in Earsham Street, later closed and pulled down and the new Post Office built on the site. At the beginning of the decade they had an overflow of boarders staying in a house in Wharton Street.

# CHAPTER 2.

## WORK AND PROSPECTS.

Although the town was small there was a very large variety of trades prospering, from the printing works who employed hundreds of workers, down to the chimney sweeps and window cleaners who worked on their own. Unfortunately at this time there was very little demand for extra labour and prospects were not very good for those out of work or the young people leaving school. Traditionally, whenever it was possible, sons would follow in their father's footsteps but when there were large families involved and times were lean as they were now, employers could not take on the extra people. There were always a certain number of men, usually the same ones, standing outside the labour exchange in Lower Olland Street on the days they had to sign on to qualify for their dole benefit.

There was very little, if any, official help for the fourteen year olds to get a steady job. Every autumn quite a number of girls starting work for the first time would be taken on by the local printer and these would replace older girls who had already left or were about to leave to be married. There would also be annual vacancies for some apprentices in various departments to maintain the quota as others completed their seven years training. These were the prime jobs that all parents would have liked to see offered to their children but unless they had a member of their family already employed there they would be very fortunate to be given a chance.

Quite a number of boys took on part time work while still at school, sometimes with a view that they might be kept on when their school days were over. Most grocers, greengrocers and other shopkeepers employed errand boys to deliver orders to their customers and this was considered a very important part of their service. People could write their order in a book supplied by the grocer and this would be put in his letter box by the husband on his way to work or one of the children when they went to school. It was then got ready by the shop assistant and duly delivered by the errand boy on a trade bicycle which had a carrier on the front and the tradesmen's name clearly marked on a plate fixed beneath the crossbar. A considerable amount of weight was often carried in this way and quite a lot of skill as well as strength was necessary to maintain balance getting on and off and negotiating uneven road surfaces. The order book, having had prices put alongside items and added up with the total clearly marked would be returned with the order to the customer who would call in during the week whenever it was convenient to settle the account. The order book signed by the cashier or a small sticky receipt stuck on the page would be the only paperwork involved as far as the customer was concerned.

Of course, not everyone did their shopping that way, some people preferred to purchase goods daily as they required them from their local shops. Even the larger stores who had full time staff depended on the schoolboys who worked for an hour or more after school and on Saturdays to do the deliveries and odd jobs such as sweeping up. Although the errand boys work was strenuous, they always seemed quite happy with their lot and those who were more efficient and considerate toward their customers were usually rewarded with refreshments, particularly in extreme weather when a hot drink was most welcome, also they could expect generous tips at such times as Easter and Christmas. One attribute they all seemed to have in common was the ability to whistle and this they did with great flair as they went cheerfully about their business, often showing a great deal of talent as they rendered their repertoire of tunes which they probably picked up from the Hollywood musicals shown at the cinema.

There were other part time jobs for the older schoolchildren but they were mostly manual and hard work. However, during the school holidays there was often a chance to supplement pocket money with more seasonal work. For the bigger and stronger there was often an opportunity to caddy for the golfers on the common at weekends when they had their tournaments. The bowls club and tennis clubs required ball boys for their special occasions and although the money was not much, it was very welcome and there was always a waiting list of youngsters willing to do these jobs.

For the adults, especially those with families these were very difficult times when even those who had regular employment found it difficult to make ends meet. Work was mostly manual with little or no call for white collar workers and where there was, such jobs were filled by those fortunate enough to have been educated at a grammar school. Generally these posts were based in the city necessitating an hour long bus ride twice a day. For younger people the starting salary was no more than would be paid to a manual worker and as much as half of it would be taken on fares but the prospects were good and as they got older and more experienced they would, of course, be very much better off.

Had there been vacancies there was a large selection of trades to choose from in the town. Besides those already mentioned there were thatchers, millers, timber merchants, corn merchants, gamekeepers, cobblers and lots more including a factory making garments from sheepskins and another employing several women and girls making snares which were made of wire and used to catch rabbits. People also worked at the maltings [there were two in the town and others just outside], on the railway or at the gas works which was always busy, with evidence of its working apparent from the tongue of flame shooting up from chimney and clearly visible to all especially at night when it was dark. By the end of the decade one or two garages had opened offering a new challenge to those who might be mechanically minded.

Conditions at the printing works were vastly different to those experienced by other workers. Both agricultural, business and shop employees had longer hours, less security and generally lower pay with little or no union power to support them, whereas the printer's workers had as many as five unions between them and these were among the strongest in the country, well capable of ensuring the best deal for their members.

Farm work was hard and those concerned with livestock were required to work seven days a week starting early in the morning and labouring until late at night. Although much of the work was skilled, men employed on the land were mostly looked upon and treated as labourers. Many of them were only part time, moving from farm to farm to help with the harvest, haymaking and pulling beet as the seasons came round. As well as these workers the smaller farmers would call on the services of such people as the hay merchant when they required trusses to be cut from his hay stack. When the hay was brought from the fields it was built into one large stack with a thatching of straw on the top to keep it dry and as it was required, the square truss was cut with a large sharp type of scythe which would be kept sharp by regular rubbing with a carborundum stone. Another tool would be used to twist loose hay and make a rope with which the truss was tied. It was essential the hay was dry before stacking otherwise internal combustion could cause it to smoulder and burn and this was quite a common occurrence especially after a wet season.

Casual labour was readily available while the economy was weak and money was short and not many businesses could afford to offer people permanent positions. There was other part time work for those fortunate enough to get it on the fruit farms when the fruit was ready to pick or at peak times with the market gardeners. Sometimes there might be an odd days work at the stables if for some reason they were extra busy at a particular time or someone on their permanent staff was away ill. In such cases they wouldn't be away too long as any sick benefit they might receive would be very much less than they earned while they were at work. There were jobs that came up regularly like cutting the weeds in the river when they had become so long they affected the flow of the millstream and there were times when the river was cleared all the way round the Common to the delight of all the anglers who no longer got their lines tangled in the weeds, the swimmers and the people who enjoyed boating.

In August when the shooting season started both men and boys would be required to go brushing to flush out the game birds so the local squire and his friends could shoot them. Besides payment for the job, if it proved to be a very successful day, all those taking part might be given a bird which would be more than acceptable when they got home. On occasions when heavy snow had fallen or there were very sharp frosty conditions the council took extra men from the dole to clear and treat the roads and pavements in the town. Such tasks were entirely manual except for the wooden snow plough which could be seen, when not in use, on the side of the road at the top of St. John's Hill. This V shaped plough was horse drawn and as it was pulled over the snow it levelled it off, pushing the surplus snow to the side where it piled up in the gutters and on the pavements.

Girls leaving school could still find work in service starting out as kitchen or chamber maids but this would usually be their last choice. It might be with an upper class family where they would possibly have to live in but there was a chance of advancement if they remained with the same household long enough or it could be with a middle class family where they would go in on a daily basis. In either case the pay was poor and the terms strict and none could expect more than a half day off each week. If there were children in the household and the maid was in favour, she might be asked to accompany the family on their annual holiday to the seaside. She would find herself with an almost full time job looking after the children so the master and mistress could come and go without any inhibitions but at least it would give her a break from her monotonous daily chores. Positions were sometimes available for a married couple without children with the woman serving as housekeeper or cook and her husband as gardener or handyman, or perhaps butler. People taking these posts were usually already employed in service when they married and intended to make it a career for life.

Every essential trade was represented in the town but being a small place many remained a one man or father and son business. Everything was made by hand and it was always intriguing to watch any one of the master tradesmen, be it the blacksmith shaping a shoe, a wheelwright or carpenter jointing a piece of wood or even a baker making bread. They were all generally pleased to demonstrate their skills. Fortunately there were still some like the builders, carpenters, bakers etc. able to take apprentices while others like the wheelwright, saddler and blacksmith saw their trades diminishing as the decade progressed and motorisation replaced the horse. Many more changes became apparent as we moved nearer to the end of the thirties and the possibility of war became more a probability. People became aware of what was going on elsewhere in this country and beyond as wireless was made more easily available to everyone and communications improved. As people realised they no longer had to settle for the meagre existence and hardships they had endured over the past years there was now so much more to look forward to. More jobs were created as things picked up and some new houses were being built on the outskirts of the town, with electricity and piped water laid on, to rehouse many of the families who had been forced to live in old inadequate and often squalid accommodation because there was nowhere else for them to go.

CHAPTER 3.


THE PEOPLE.


*THE WORKING CLASS.*
   The popular saying, 'a women's place is in the home' was much used and meant as very few working class women went out to work after they were married and most of those that did had professional careers. It was generally accepted that girls left their employment after their wedding and devoted all of their time to making a home and subsequently bringing up a family. Wages being low, they would have to save up every penny they could and all over the age of about eighteen would be happy to accept birthday and Christmas presents which were suitable for their 'bottom drawer' while they themselves would always be on the lookout for linen or trinkets which they would like to have in their new home. Although there were many traditions like the brides father paying for the wedding reception, in these times they often had to be waived as he was unable to afford them. The first problem a couple had was finding a place to live and this would have to be rented as no working class man could afford to buy his own house. He was fortunate if between them they were able to furnish a couple of rooms with second hand furniture and bits and

pieces given to them by friends and neighbours. Sometimes accommodation was available from the man's employer. Farmers in particular provided a house for their permanent workers which meant they could pay them less and they had little chance of finding alternative accommodation if they left. Other employers who were able to, like the printing works, followed the farmers example. However in that particular instance, things were so bad during this period they had to sell some of their houses with their employees still occupying them to help meet urgent financial commitments.

In spite of all the drawbacks couples, no matter how poor, managed to get married in a church with bridesmaids and the full regalia and with a reception to follow to make it a day for all to remember. For girls in particular, the wedding day was considered the most important day in her life and all friends and relations would rally round to do their best to make sure it was. Most marriages took place at the weekend and the bridegroom would have to return to work on Monday unless it was his holiday week and in any case, no one could afford to take time off and very few had a honeymoon. Wedding dresses were often handed on from mother to daughter or borrowed for the day, while the new suit bought by the groom for the occasion would be the only one he had in a very long time. Before the big day the bride-to-be would spend much of her time making curtains and anything else she could for the new home, usually with her mother's help. Mats made by passing pieces of cut up rags through a hessian base were popular. They cost little to make and as floors were covered with lino, if at all, rugs and mats were needed on the hearth, beside the bed and anywhere else they would add to warmth and comfort.

Some of the older houses had bare brick floors downstairs which had to be scrubbed, while upstairs there would be bare boards. The lino covering which was commonly used was quite thin with a kind of tar on the back and very easily torn when being put down or taken up. There was a large selection of colours and designs as well as quality to choose from but unfortunately the cheaper ones took very little time for the pattern to wear off in the places were it was most walked on so it was often better to choose something in a plain colour.

There was a lot of difference in the fortunes of individuals among the working class and the renumeration received did not always reflect the effort required to get it. Farm workers and the like had a hard life for a meagre reward and people like shop assistants who worked less hours also received very poor pay. There were others in work getting even less money for their labours while at the other end of the ladder people like the printers were doing much better. With the odd few hours of overtime they enjoyed the security of a job for life and, the tradesmen at least, must have been the highest paid workers in the town. Those worst off were the men who found themselves out of work through no fault of their own but as a result of the economic state of the country. They had set their living standards to match the income they were receiving and found it extremely difficult to adjust and manage on the pittance paid by the dole. Like all towns and villages there were a number of men, some with families, who never really wanted to work and never would if they could get out of it. In these cases, as in most others where there was a family, it was the women and children who suffered most.

These days running a home was a full time job even with a small family, although it was said that in larger families the children all looked after each other, the parents concerned might not agree. In cooler weather the day started with the wood being brought in and a fire lit for water to be heated for an early morning cup of tea. At other times when it was warmer an oil stove might be used. Washing first thing had to be done in cold water taken from the tap if there was one or from a bucket if you depended on a pump when it was poured into a bowl using a jug. Where they had facilities in the larger houses this would be done in the bedroom using the jug and bowl which stood on a marble topped washstand. After use the dirty water had to be tipped into another bucket and thrown outside. Many times in a day the bucket of fresh water would need refilling from the tap or pump and this chore would mostly fall on the housewife. On Monday mornings the copper had to be filled to heat the water for the weekly wash and this would often be rainwater taken from a tub or cistern where it had been collected from the roof. This was preferred to the treated tap water as it was softer and easy to lather which meant far less soap was used. Water was always used sparingly from the pumps, not only because it had to be fetched but because at times of drought the springs and pumps were likely to dry up and there would be even further to go to fetch it. So unless there was an inside tap that made life so much easier, whenever it was possible there was good reason to use rainwater for the weekly wash and bathing.

All dirty linen was saved for the one weekly wash so it was a long and hard task. After washing, the water had to be changed for rinsing, this would most likely be done in cold water, then, unless you were one of the very fortunate who owned a mangle, everything had to be wrung out by hand before being hung on a line in the back garden or small back yard then propped up to take the largest items clear of the ground and make the most of the wind to dry them. During fine weather it might all be dried on that same day but when the weather was bad the wet linen would have to be hung indoors or dried on a clothes horse around the fire. Normal daily housework and preparing the dinner had to be done between washes because the children and perhaps the man of the house would be home for their meal at mid-day. Then followed the job of ironing which was done with a flat iron, heated in the fire, picked up with tongs and inserted into a case. The heat was tested by licking a finger and lightly touching the bottom. Hopefully all would be ironed and aired by Tuesday night but this depended on the weather for in the summer much of the airing was done outside in the sunshine and in the winter, if it was really cold, the family would huddle round the fire so there was no room for the clothes horse.

Another day, possibly Thursday, would be the day set aside for baking and unless you had an oil oven or cooking range so the existing fire heated the oven, another fire would have to be lit. The amount of cakes, buns and scones etc. made depended on the size of the family and also on their income but all would have some even if it was only bread and butter pudding or plain scones.

Bath night was likely to be on Friday and it had to be planned to suit the whole family. The copper was filled, the fire lit, and the tin bath brought in from outside where it was kept hanging on the wall or in the garden shed. It was unlikely there would be sufficient hot water for everyone to have it clean so smaller children would go in together and others would follow in turn with one getting in as another got out and at the same time a little more water was added from the copper to keep it hot. When all had bathed it would take two to carry the bath outside and empty it, otherwise it had to be baled out into a pail using a hand basin.

Working class families generally were quite large and couples seemed to have their first child soon after getting married so it is easy to see how the housewife soon became trapped in a full time job keeping the home together and attending to the every need of husband and children. The only sex education girls could expect was what they were told by their mother or picked up from other girls. Boys got their knowledge from their companions by word of mouth and for both sexes it was generally in the form of a joke which would be quickly passed on. Nevertheless by the age of ten most children had a very good idea of what it was all about. The fact they lived in the country meant many things which had to be taught to children in the large towns were seen and accepted by country children who observed natural animal life from the time they could walk and talk. The only reference to the subject of sex made by many parents to their sons when they were in their teens, was something like, 'you had better not bring any trouble home here!'.

The consequence of all this was that few young people were aware of the facts of birth control and after they were married, not many took serious steps to exercise it. French letters were available but only from small independent chemists [the large chain stores did not stock them] or the barber where they could be purchased with a wink or nod when a haircut or shave were being paid for. These were quite expensive for anyone out of work or in a low paid job.

There were, as always, instances of young unmarried women and even schoolgirls becoming pregnant. In cases where the couple were too young or for some other reason could not be married it was quite a common practice for the child to be brought up by the girl's parents as a member of their family while she, after a short time, resumed her life where she left off. Very often when she married the child remained with her parents. Sometimes the grandparents helped out by bringing up the oldest child when there was a large family and they were struggling to make ends meet.

It was a constant worry for working class parents to find the money to feed and clothe their families and it was usual for garments to be passed on to younger members of the family as the older children grew out of them. Many at this time were dependent on clothes given them or those they bought at jumble sales. They would also be on the lookout for any material suitable for cutting and sewing to use in the home. Boys wore short trousers just above the knees until they were about fourteen or fifteen years old and it was not unusual to see them with the lining hanging out of holes worn in the seat, while a glance at the feet might show a pair of badly worn shoes which could have been second hand to start with. It was quite a common practice for both adults and children to put a piece of thick cardboard inside the shoe to cover a hole in the sole.

For married women the family came first so their own wardrobe was made up largely of clothes they had acquired or made themselves, consequently they were usually dressed in dull or dark colours and the style of their clothes was quite plain. They did wear a pinafore when they were working in the house which was sleeveless and sometimes colourful, this was put on like a coat with one side crossed over the other in the front, then held in place by strings tied round the waist. To keep the hair clean while they worked or to conceal curlers a scarf was wrapped around the head and secured on the top with a bow to give the appearance of a turban.

Men chose their clothes, when they were able, to be durable rather than for appearance and would go for hard wearing cords or tweeds. They always had a wide leather belt, not necessarily to hold up their trousers for this was done by braces which passed through loops on the waist of their long johns before being fastened to the trouser buttons to hold them up. Shirts were made of flannel with buttons at the neck so they had to be pulled over the head to put them on. They had separate collars and there were two for each shirt if they were required but as a collar and tie would only be worn on very special occasions most shirts were purchased without them. It was possible to buy separate white collars, soft or starched in all sizes and these like the others were held at the back and front by studs. Some soft collars had slots underneath the points at the front into which thin plastic strips were put to stop them curling up. These strips were a product made from milk and must have been among the first plastic type articles to be used. They had to be removed when the collar was washed or they went all crinkly. Another alternative was to buy paper collars which could be worn a couple of times and then thrown away. The shirts were long, reaching well down the thigh with a slightly longer tail at the back, this was wrapped between the legs before the trousers were pulled on. Probably being one of only two owned it was most likely worn for a week, depending on what work was done, then changed on bath night. This same shirt might also serve as night attire. The popular headgear worn by men was a soft cap with a snap holding the peak up, although as the decade passed, many younger people being influenced by the Hollywood films had started wearing a trilby when they went out after work was finished.

Girls also followed the fashion trends and got ideas from the cinema which was a good incentive for them to learn to be proficient with a needle and thread and with mother's help they invariably managed to look their best. Their very first priority after starting work was to have pretty clothes to wear in the evenings and for socialising. Towards the latter half of the decade fashions became brighter and more colourful and there was a larger selection of styles. If you were going out for the evening a pair of silk stockings were essential. It also became fashionable for girls to have their eyebrows plucked to leave just a thin line which was emphasised with a black pencil and in some cases they completely removed the eyebrows and depended entirely on the pencil line. All kinds of make-up was now available from the chemists and practically all girls and young women used cleansing or foundation creams as well as powder, lipstick and rouge to create their own personal complexion. For most, a regular visit to the hairdresser was too expensive and they styled their hair themselves at home. Before going to bed or after washing the hair small pieces of rag, bandage or even pipe cleaners were tied at the end of a section of hair which was then rolled up and secured by tying the two ends around the bundle it had formed in a bow so it was easily untied in the morning. There were available various kinds of tongs designed for curling the hair. These had to be heated in the fire or over the gas to just the correct heat before clamping onto the end of a section of hair and rolling it up. This then had to be held until the tongs cooled then unrolled and the process repeated until all the head was done. Unfortunately the only way to test how hot the curler was, was the same method used on the iron when ironing and the slightest misjudgment could have disastrous consequences.

There is no doubt that during the hardships of the 1930's the poor suffered most and of those the women folk were the worst off. No matter how bad things became the men always seemed to find sufficient money for cigarettes and beer. It was still officially claimed smoking was good for you especially for the relief of tension and it was mainly the men who indulged in it. Very few women smoked and those that enjoyed a drink had to settle for a bottle being brought home when the husband came from the pub as it was not acceptable for ladies to frequent public bars. Racing was followed daily by a lot of men and although it was not legal bookie's runners operated taking bets in many workplaces and pubs and as so often is the case, the people who could least afford to gamble were the very ones who did it most. Perhaps those who have little or nothing feel they have nothing to lose and realise too late the consequences when they have nothing left with which to buy food or pay the rent. This would leave them with two alternatives, they could borrow money from a money lender at a very high interest rate which gave them no chance of clearing the debt for a very long time, or, if they had anything of value, they could take it to the local pawnbroker with little chance of seeing it again. Either of these choices was a step toward having the bailiff sent in. This action was taken when creditors had, after a reasonable time, given up any hope of having the debt settled. The bailiff moved into the house to ensure nothing was sold or disposed of before the creditor was able to pick the articles to auction in order to settle the account. If it was a large amount of money, all the family's possessions put together would not raise enough and they would lose everything. Then, if they were unable to pay the rent they were evicted, an action always carried out with the police in attendance.

As always with gambling not many people won and in the long run the one to suffer most was the wife trying to keep the home together. Married women did not very often accompany their husbands when they went out. It would have to be a special event and then it was likely the whole family would go together. So it could not have been a very happy time for women of the working class and yet most of them, even if not content, did not seem to let it get them down. They had the expected disagreements with their neighbours but they also spent happy hours together, laughing and discussing the news of the day. Beyond that they depended on each other at time of need and knew that whatever happened there was someone to back them up and lend a hand.

It was difficult enough to house and cloth the family but when money was so short feeding them was an even bigger problem. The food they had was plain but wholesome, meat was very expensive but from Spring through to Autumn vegetables were plentiful and many families had at least a small garden or allotment where they could grow some their own. Flour was not too dear and traditional cooking meant there would be a good selection of savoury and sweet puddings. With a few bones, dried peas and potatoes, a nourishing and tasty pea soup was ready in a couple of hours to be eaten with steamed suet dumplings. At times, particularly harvest, rabbits were available and many men went to catch them themselves, putting down snares or using a ferret and digging them out. Otherwise one could be bought for a few pence and would provide an excellent meal for it was equally good baked, stewed or in a pie.

During the herring season people like the bus crews on regular trips to Lowestoft and Gt. Yarmouth would go down to the quay where they were in abundance and cheap and bring back bags full which they passed on to friends and neighbours. Milk was easily available and an important part of people's diet but too expensive to be used extravagantly. A popular breakfast for manual workers who could afford it was bread and milk. For those who had to take a packed meal to work, bread and American red cheese was what most found in their lunch boxes and if the baking had been done there would be  a short cake or scone to go with it. The mainstay to curb the children's appetite was bread and jam. A stock of jam was likely to have been made when the fruit was ripe and available. This was yet another chore added to the wife's duties.

There was little people could do to improve their living standards and they seemed to resign themselves to accept things as they were. Recognising their place in society they always looked up to and showed respect for the members of the classes above them addressing them at all times as 'sir' or by name and being ever ready to step one side and 'doff' their cap whenever they met or passed in the street. These actions were copied by the children who were taught basic manners at school but had little chance of learning much about etiquette and what was considered good manners in their own homes where the necessary facilities were so limited. However most parents did their best and each had their own methods of teaching children right from wrong and how to behave in public.

A LIFE LONG FARM WORKER

## THE MIDDLE CLASS.

In a small market town the middle class were said to be the backbone of the community. Generally they kept themselves to themselves but there was always the odd one or two individuals from a working class background who managed through hard work and endeavour to educate themselves and move up but it was not easy to get accepted and they had to be careful not to disagree with senior members of various bodies or their life might be made very difficult. Although it was absolutely necessary to have sufficient income to claim class status a high standard of manners and bearing still had to be apparent and exercised for some time before their acceptance was assured.

Some of the shopkeepers and businessmen had their living accommodation at the same location as their work and there were advantages living over the shop or adjoining the workshop. However, the premises were generally quite old and lacked facilities and comfort besides which appearances were very important so many chose to live on the outskirts of the town in such places as Wingfield Street, Flixton Road and Outney Road. The houses were usually quite large even though some were terraced, they were mostly owner occupied and very few of them were rented. At the start of the decade there were not many with modern conveniences, flush toilets were generally situated outside the main buildings and electric lights were only just being put in. Although some had the luxury of gas for both heating and lighting it was usual to have lights installed only in those rooms which were constantly in use, like the drawing room, dining room, kitchen and perhaps the master bedroom. The light given off by the gas mantle even when turned up high was poor and in no way compared with electricity. Water pumps were still to be found over a small shallow sink in some kitchens while others had water piped to a single tap. By this time the larger houses owned by the more affluent did have bathrooms with the water piped to gas heaters or coke fired boilers. In some houses where the water was still heated in the copper in the kitchen it was pumped to the bath in the bathroom upstairs using a pump which had to be operated by hand.

Daily routine in the household was very strict and children were brought up to adhere to it. Punctuality and good manners were essential if an example was to be set for others to follow so adults were always on time and expected everyone else to be the same for people were judged by the way they were seen to conduct themselves. Ever aware of this both men and women took great care with their appearance and did their best to uphold the highest moral standards whenever they were in the public eye or with their children. They remained aloof from their employees and would sometimes communicate with junior members of their staff only through the manager or foreman. Position on the social ladder was very important to them, so much so that in some cases it became almost a competition between families which led to a good deal of jealousy and back biting. However on issues involving people outside their class and small circle of friends they always stood firmly together.

Children attended preparatory school from the age of five and then went on to grammar school when they were ten. During all of this time they would dress in the appropriate uniform when the emphasis on good behaviour experienced at home was compounded by the school who had it's own high standards. It is not surprising that parents used their children to score points against each other especially if they had an exceptionally bright child or one who had outstanding skills in a particular sport or pastime. The one time they were able to promote themselves to full advantage was at a daughter's wedding when no expense was spared. The betrothed would have a similar background [or better] and meet with the approval of the whole family. The wedding and reception was expected to be the very best the parents were able to afford not only to give the bride a day to remember but to make it an event everyone would remember. There had to be a shopping spree to buy dresses for the bride, bridesmaids, page and of course, a new outfit for mother and new suit for father. Then there was the honeymoon to be booked. Generally a busy and exciting time for all but fathers must have often counted their blessings that, on average, their families were confined to two children and they must have felt even better if at least one of theirs was a boy.

As in all walks of life there were some families on the bottom of the ladder and others near the top, with a corresponding difference in their financial standing. But one thing they all seemed to have in common was that something which drove them to almost any length in order to appear better off than their neighbours. The more affluent employed domestic staff in their homes. Sometimes just a young single girl as a maid to do the general cleaning, that is all the dirtier jobs like blacking the stove, clearing out the ashes or emptying the slops [this still had to be done for while lavatories remained outside people required chamber pots under the bed which had to be emptied and washed out daily]. It was more prestigious to employ a housekeeper to run the house and help with the cooking and washing as well as the maid but this was expensive and a good compromise would be to employ an older woman, who's children were off hand, as a part time housekeeper. This was one of the few opportunities for a working class woman to work later in life and although the pay was not too good, if they had the job for some time, and many did, they became trusted and well thought of and would be rewarded in many other ways. For instance, they could take home any food left over and from time to time items of clothing or household goods which were replaced or discarded were given to them for their own family's use. Also it was often useful to have influential contacts.

If there were young children in the family a full or part time nanny might be taken on. No matter who applied for these domestic posts, to be successful they required very good character references and be presented clean, well mannered and humble and any association other members of the family might have with anyone known to the potential employer was always a big help. Children were discouraged and sometimes forbidden to associate with the servants and speaking to them only when it was necessary but after some time when there was no doubt the servant knew her place, trust grew and it was not unknown for them to be entrusted to escort the children to school or to play when the parents were otherwise committed.

In their shops and workplaces the men were easily discernable by their dress for all, except those smaller businessmen who donned their trade aprons, wore dark suits with buttoned waistcoats and a watch with a gold chain stretched across from pocket to pocket and some, no matter whether indoors or outside, would wear a hard bowler hat. Walking to work in wet weather a large black umbrella would be put up to keep the rain off it and a pair of galoshes pulled over their shoes so the splashing from puddles did not blur the shine. On really cold days some might even sport a pair of spats which buttoned around the ankles and could be bought in all sorts of designs and colours. Socks were held up securely over the legs of long pants by suspenders but in warmer weather the long pants were exchanged for combinations which were vest and short pants combined, they buttoned up all down the front and were put on by pulling them onto your legs before putting your arms into the sleeves and buttoning the front. A reasonably large slit was built in at the back so there was no need to completely undress when it was necessary to go to the lavatory.

The middle classes, like their betters, were proud of their jewellry and accessories. Many had gold rings on their fingers and cuff links holding their shirt sleeves which were held up by arm bands to ensure they were just the right length to show below the jacket sleeves. Tie pins and clips, always acceptable as presents, were popular and it was usual for some to complete their dress with a flower in their buttonhole or a handkerchief folded neatly into a point protruding out of their breast pocket. A regular daily visit to the barber for a shave was a practice followed and enjoyed by many not too far up the social ladder for it was the barber who was relied on to glean and pass on news and information. Beards were not at all popular but many were proud to sport a moustache and a growing number of younger men liked them small and thin, [based on those worn by the hollywood stars], but most were worn thick and bushy, walrus style, requiring a trim only every couple of weeks or so.

It was mainly from these people that the Town's Electorate choose those they wished to represent them on the Council and various governing bodies. The women as well as the men gave up their time to serve on committees and it must be said it was as a result of the efforts of their predecessors that Bungay was prosperous. Of course being elected Town Reeve or Chairman of the Council could only be good for business but all seeking such posts would deny most emphatically that their canvassing had any such motivation. Those who were elected or volunteered for such duties served the town well although their efforts were not always appreciated by everyone. Although satisfying, such jobs were very time consuming and often costly, especially for those like the Town Reeve who, being responsible for various trusts and charities, would be expected to lead by example when launching an appeal for one of them. This he was obliged to do if he was to leave his mark when his term of office came to an end.

The women undertook many of the tasks involved in running the church or chapel committees, organising the fund raising and running the events as well as taking on the duties of cleaning and flower arranging etc. in the churches. A few also took their places beside the men on the Town Council, the school's Governors, Justices of the Peace and other important bodies. Compared to the working class the middle class men and women lived quite well although they too were affected by the hard times. While they occupied themselves in their spare time with their social work, their pleasures were mainly derived from mixing with colleagues and neighbours at the many functions they organised when they would be on the lookout to try to score points against each other. Some managed to find time for a round or two of golf on the common or pass away an hour or so on the bowling green and most enjoyed a walk out with the family on a Sunday. On a visit to the local pub they would take a seat in the smoke room away from the noise and smoke of the public bar where they would meet others of the same status. The women would certainly not accompany them for they would consider it degrading to be seen there. Most pubs had a slip bar where you could enter unobserved to buy bottled beer and cigarettes to take away. Most men in this class who enjoyed an alcoholic drink would usually have it in the privacy of their own home, at the golf house or in one of the hotels.

There was no shortage of good food if you could afford it and these people lived well with a balanced diet. Perhaps the children, who were expected to eat what was put in front of them did not always appreciate how fortunate they were. It is true they were not allowed sweets and chocolate except on special occasions and then only in moderation as it was recognised how bad they were for their teeth but they would have at least three meals a day and for some it was four if afternoon tea was included. For main meals meat or fish accompanied by vegetables in season would be followed with home made dishes of fruit often cased in crust. Variety depended on the skill of the cook who might be the housekeeper or the lady of the house herself but, whichever it was, all enjoyed the pies and creative cooking which was an essential skill passed down from mother to daughter. The women did not often go into the local shops, their orders were placed and the goods delivered.

To purchase their clothes they would most likely take a trip to the city where there was a much larger choice and they were able to keep up with the latest trends not only in clothes but such things as make-up and beauty treatment for it was essential they always looked their best and they were quite willing to bear a great deal of discomfort to do so. Even in the warmest weather they held their figures in with large laced up corsets containing long flexible steel strips running up and down all the way round with suspenders attached to the bottom to hold their stockings up. They chose their shoes for appearance and style rather than comfort or practicability so they were often too tight with heels too high resulting in corns and blisters. Visits to the local hairdresser for a permanent wave followed by a regular wash and set ensured that their hair was always neat and tidy and a new hat was a must for every special occasion that had to be attended.

The worst of their household chores were done for them and it seemed life was kind and yet they never seemed to be able to relax. Maintaining high standards at all times in the home was difficult. Everything had to be spotlessly clean, the table laid for meals with each place set with everything in it's own exact position. Each person had their own serviette folded, rolled neatly and placed in a personal silver ring, this would be removed and placed on the lap before the meal was started and replaced before leaving the table when it was finished. The children were at the table before their parents entered the dining room and they would remain silent throughout the meal unless spoken to or it was really necessary to say something, when they had finished eating they awaited permission before leaving the table. At all times during the meal constant watch was kept to ensure everyone held their knife and fork correctly, tilted their plate away when eating the last of their soup, placing their cutlery correctly when they had eaten all they wanted etc.

They were repeatedly reminded of the responsibility they had to maintain the high standard of behaviour required to protect the family name. Their daily routine was mapped out for them and the friends they chose to associate with during their leisure hours were selected from a small number of nominees approved by the parents. These children were taught their manners by example at home where they were safe and secure but in their determination to bring them up to follow in their own footsteps adults often overlooked the need for understanding and love. Consequently there were instances when these children, away from the eyes of their parents, would revolt and not only ignore the code they had been taught but act defiantly in a most rude and sometimes obscene manner. Unfortunately in many cases where this happened the parents never became aware of it.

## THE UPPER CLASS.

The halls and manors set on their estates on the outskirts of the town and villages were the homes of these people who were rarely seen but constantly talked about. They usually held some high office with or without a title and would preside over the more prestigious local committee or charity where the association with their name was sufficient to encourage the more influential people to become involved. The large homes and estates provided employment for people from other classes and those who worked for them were highly respected among their own class, particularly those like the gamekeeper who was always the centre of attraction in the local pub. The general public were always hungry for any snippets of news involving their superiors and who better to get it from than an employee who was sometimes involved in events taking place and had constant contact with the servants who could have had little other than the family to talk about when they got together at the end of the day after their work was done. The staff might have been able to get a good idea of how they lived and conducted their private lives but as far as business matters were concerned, they kept these to themselves. The size of the house, the acreage of the estate and perhaps the number of farms and houses they owned was common knowledge but beyond that the most that anyone could say was that they spend most of their time in London or perhaps just that they were away. People soon learned to accept this.

There were no more than two or three of these families living in the confines of the town itself and had more wanted to settle here they would have been unlikely to find accommodation with enough large rooms or in a sufficiently secluded setting which was suitable and in keeping with their status. There were those at the top end of the middle class who tended to stick together in a position aloof and devoid of feeling for, or interest in any one else at all. They thought they were in a class above their fellows, when in reality they were a very long way from ever achieving the status or respect or just as important, the necessary finance required to meet the commitment borne by the upper class.

# CHAPTER 4.

## TRANSPORT.

We were still in the age of steam and the railways did most of the transporting of goods and people around the country. The Waveney Valley line was owned by the London and North Eastern Railway Company and ran from Beccles to Tivetshall where it connected with the Norwich to Liverpool Street main line. This was a single track and up and down trains crossed at Bungay. There they would wait at the platform until the signalman came down from his signal box to take the staff which was the 'key' for the track they had just run over and give them the one just taken from the driver of the train on the other platform. This confirmed to him the line ahead was clear as there was only one staff for each section of single track. As soon as the driver had the correct staff a blast on a whistle and the waving of a green flag by the guard was all that was required for him to open the regulator and force noisy puffs of smoke out of the chimney as the engine's wheels slowly turned and the train began to move. The puffs got quicker as the speed increased and the 'clickety-clack' noise made by the wheels as they passed over the joins in the rail became louder and more rhythmical. The train did not travel very fast because the distance between the stations on this line was too small to allow it to gather much speed before the brakes had to be applied to slow it down ready to stop as it came up to the platform. There were four stations between Bungay and Tivetshall and three between Bungay and Beccles where connection was made with the Ipswich to Lowestoft and Great Yarmouth line.

The service was so regular people in the town checked their clocks and watches when they heard the whistle and increasing noise as the train approached the crossings before it came into the station. All of the crossings were manned and the person responsible for opening and closing the gates each time a train went through lived in a house alongside them which had been built exclusively for his use. This was considered essential as his services were required both day and night. Although every precaution was taken there were still instances of trains crashing through closed gates, but fortunately not many.

The first train of the day, often referred to as the milk train, would also bring in the the daily newspapers and early morning mail. The milk was transported in large round urns which were wide at the bottom and narrow at the top, the same as those carried by the milkman on his cart. These were moved around in the guard's van and out onto a barrow on the platform by tipping them about thirty degrees onto one side and rolling them along by turning the top, a feat made to look easy by all who handled them. Besides the dairymen and newsagents, the postmen would be there to meet this and almost every train to collect the letters and parcels which were loaded up and pushed to the post office for sorting on their familiar red hand barrows. The station was a hive of activity at such times but there was always a few minutes to spare for a quick smoke and a chat before the train arrived when everyone went about their business as quickly as they could. Other than in the middle of summer it always seemed to be very cold on the station which was very much open to the wind blowing up the Waveney Valley. There was a large waiting room with a big dark brown table in the centre [the type found in all railway waiting rooms] and strong wooden benches painted the same colour positioned all around the walls. A mirror hung over the fireplace where the porter would build a fire which seemed totally inadequate to heat such a large space. No doubt this room was cleaned regularly but as with the seats on the platform, nobody would chance sitting without first putting down a newspaper or handkerchief because there was always a very good chance of them being covered in greasy black soot which seemed to cover everything that came in the vicinity of the steam trains. The booking office, which adjoined the station master's office, was usually the warmest place and passengers buying their tickets at the small hatch as they came into the station could see an inviting fire blazing away as the cold draught from outside blew around their legs. Only a privileged few were allowed through that door to warm themselves before going about their duties.

A large variety of goods were transported under the watchful eye of the guard. As well as the ordinary urgent packages which could be met off the train, goods for the shops and businesses as well as individuals were delivered to their door by the railway. It was quite usual to see small animals and pets including such things as goats, chickens and rabbits in the guard's van and the station where they awaited collection. Greyhounds, with muzzles, kept warm in coloured coats which were wrapped round their backs and secured under their chests with straps, standing with their tails curled between their legs and pigeons in crates on their way to the starting point of a race were regular passengers on this and many other lines. These were all well fed and cared for during the journey and there is no doubt some guards appreciated their company. They were not so well disposed toward the boxes of fish they often carried from the coastal towns which left wet patches wherever they had been put down and smelt as if the fish was still there.

It was only the small and urgent goods which were transported by passenger trains, the bulk was taken by goods train and unloaded at the goods station conveniently situated at the end of

Broad Street. Here there were loading bays to accommodate all kinds of goods and materials which could be handled no matter if they were in bags or loose, like grain or coal. Local coal merchants weighed, bagged and loaded their carts daily at the station taking their coal from a stock pile as it was required. There was a book stall on the platform selling newspapers, books, magazines, sweets and chocolate etc. and on the down platform there were slot machines where you inserted one penny for a bar of chocolate, two pence for five cigarettes in a paper packet and another which gave two cigarettes for a penny in a cardboard packet. The latter was very popular with younger boys who didn't often have more than a penny to spend and if they had, they were too young to go in a shop to buy cigarettes.

Tickets issued for all journeys were made of tough green cardboard, no more than two inches long by an inch wide with one half for the outward trip and the other for the return. They were scored down the centre where they were torn in half by the ticket collector who would retain the outward half on arrival at the destination. Unfortunately they did not tear easily and much bending back and forth was often necessary before the two halves separated. It cost one penny for a platform ticket obtainable from a machine or the ticket office if you wished to see someone off or meet them on the platform when the train pulled into the station. Tickets were available for dogs and pets which accompanied passengers in their carriage and also for things like bicycles, prams and pushchairs which would be transported in the guard's van and collected from the guard at the end of the journey.

Many men were employed on the railway doing all kinds of different jobs and it was generally assumed if you were taken on when you left school you had a job for life and would retire with a pension, having first received a gold watch for twenty-five and fifty years service respectively. The footplate men were the envy of most, not only were they the best paid with what was probably the most responsible job but nearly everyone expressed a wish to drive a train at some time in their lives and, although a dirty job with very unsocial hours, it was still considered to be a glamourous one. At the end of a journey it was not unusual to see a number of passengers pause on their way as they passed the engine to have a few friendly words with the driver. All the station staff from the station master down were held in quite high regard by the general public who were all certain to make a call on their services at some time. As well as the staff who were constantly in the public eye there were the signal engineers and other tradesmen like the platelayers who were responsible for the maintenance of the track and keeping the points greased. Then there was the shunters who ensured the right carriage or wagon was in the proper place and on the correct line when it was required and many others right down to the boys who trimmed and cleaned the lamps and filled them with oil ready for when darkness fell.

Special trains and excursions were run whenever required for events such as the annual sunday school outing to Lowestoft when, instead of having to cross the platform and change trains at Beccles as people usually did, the train was shunted on to the other line while the passengers remained in their carriages. In the latter part of the decade excursions from the Waveney Valley ran to Great Yarmouth on Saturday evenings, leaving Bungay at four thirty and returning from Southtown Station at about midnight at a cost of around nine pence return. Special trains were also put on to connect with excursions which ran from Norwich to Liverpool Street station on certain Sundays. This would connect at Tivetshall and the return fare from Bungay was about six shillings and sixpence. As the train stopped at most stations it was a slow ride leaving Bungay at around seven thirty in the morning it arrived some five hours later and commenced the return journey from London at about seven thirty in the evening. All of these specials excursions seemed to be well supported.

It was toward the end of the decade when they experimented using a combined engine and carriage to give a more efficient and frequent service on this line, this was still steam driven and capable of pushing or pulling so it did not have to be turned at the end of each journey. There was probably a correct name for it but it was referred to by the locals as the 'Chevvy Chase'. However it was not used for long and it was said that it was held responsible for a number of corn fields catching fire from the sparks which, at times, flew in all directions from any steam engine but even more so from this one. These were clearly visible as they showered from the chimney, especially in the dark, as the train left the station gathering speed with the glare from the fire, shining through the open fire box door, lighting up the whole cab as the fireman shovelled in the coal to keep steam up.

Everyone depended on the railway for one reason or another and it performed an important function. Nevertheless steam trains were dirty, very noisy and because of the facilities and space required the stations had to be situated on the outskirts of the town leaving passengers with a long walk, possibly with luggage, before and after their journey and in some villages this could be a very long way. As it travelled along between stops the engine left a trail of smoke and often smuts covering the dwellings and gardens on the side of the track which must have been a constant worry on wash days when the linen was hanging outside to dry. In the station the warmth of the engine could be felt if you stood on the platform beside it and there was a constant hissing as steam seemed to be escaping from several different places giving the impression it was in a hurry to be off. An extra large gush of steam was expelled on occasions when the fireman put on the feed to top up the boiler with water. If the wind was in the wrong direction as the train travelled along it would not be possible to have the windows open without filling the compartment with smoke. On all doors there was a notice warning passengers not to put their head out of the window. Obviously they could be struck by a passing train, hit a post or some other object alongside the track. There was another reason for with sparks flying from the engine there was a good chance of getting one in your eye, something known to have happened on more than one occasion, particularly to children.

The area was well covered with a good bus service, the bulk of it undertaken by the Eastern Counties Bus Company which connected every village and hamlet. Routes between the large towns and city had double decked vehicles at peak times and were well supported by people going to and from work. On return journeys it was sometimes necessary to be early and queue to be sure of a seat and at such times only a limited number of about eight passengers were allowed to stand downstairs with none at all upstairs. Unless there were sufficient people left behind and there was a crew available no relief would be put on which meant the unlucky passengers had to wait anything up to an hour or sometimes more, before the next one was due.

The journey from Bungay to Norwich took about an hour so anyone with a job in the city not only had the extra expense of fares but also an additional two hours plus added to their working day. Like so many other things it was something they had to get used to and through the years a friendship built among the regulars which helped to make the trip more tolerable. Every bus had a conductor as well as a driver who always managed somehow to collect all the fares and sort out all the change as well as count the passengers and record the numbers between each stop before it reached it's destination. With the bus crowded and people standing, the first passengers he attended to never seemed to have the correct money so he had to remember to return to them with their change before they got off. It was a job calling for a clear head and calm temperament and although it was some help to him that regulars had season tickets which only had to be looked at, there were times when he was further obstructed by an Inspector getting on to check all tickets.

Although only single decker vehicles were used on the country routes they were still much too large for the roads and meeting another bus or lorry going in the opposite direction was a hazard they were often confronted with. Slow moving horse drawn carts were a problem for the driver no matter if they were coming towards him or he came up from behind to pass them. In either case the narrow roads made it impossible for him to pass in many places and he had to be ever wary of the soft verges and ditches that were to be found on the side of many of the roads. High banks topped with hedges and trees with branches hanging out over the road were another hazard for the driver to look out for and it was not unusual, even on the main roads, to have part of the hedgerow brush down the nearside when the driver had to pull over or to hear the swish and scratching of an overhanging tree as it scraped across the roof. It is hardly surprising journeys were often quite slow. In the winter things were even more difficult when there had been heavy rain to wash mud from the fields onto the roads or a severe frost to give an icy surface perhaps accompanied by fog. At such times narrow country roads really were hazardous.

There were a number of private companies who ran regular daily trips but these were not allowed to operate where they were in direct competition with the Eastern Counties. However they offered a good and often essential service to many of the more remote places and ran frequent excursions to the seaside in the summer, giving people the opportunity to see places which were otherwise difficult to reach. In the winter they organised expeditions to the shops, especially at the time of the sales and as christmas approached. The local senior football teams depended on these coaches to transport them for their away fixtures on Saturday afternoons and other organisations booked them for their annual outings.

The Eastern Counties Bus Company provided a small parcel service between the towns and goods could be left for delivery or collected from the wool shop in the Market Place who acted as agent for them. At the bus station in Norwich they had a parcels office where they were all sorted and if necessary, transferred to other vehicles which would take them on to their destination. At Bungay the bus stopped outside the shop and the conductor took in the parcels he had for delivery and picked up any awaiting despatch. If there was room, he stacked them out of the way under the stairs but if there was not, he put them onto the luggage rack where they always had to go on the single deck buses anyway as there was nowhere else for them. Dogs were allowed to travel on all buses so long as they were escorted and the person in charge of them bought them a ticket. They were only allowed downstairs on double deckers.

The bicycle played an important part in many peoples lives and was used as a means of transport by many as they went about their daily duties as well those who needed it to get them to work. Constantly in use it needed regular maintenance to keep it in good order and this was quite costly when it came to things like new tyres or a chain. Most repairs, especially common ones like a puncture, people did themselves and every cycle owner kept a few spanners and tools handy with a puncture repair kit which was usually carried in a small leather bag strapped to the back of the saddle. The repair shops in the town did quite well for even those who were able to do the work themselves still had to buy the parts. Unfortunately a large number of people with their own cycles could not afford to or just didn't bother to keep them in tip top order and many rode with unadjusted brakes and worn blocks, sometimes they had only one brake and that was on the front wheel which meant steep hills had to be negotiated with both feet scraping on the road to prevent the bike going out of control.

After dark it was compulsory to have a light on the front and a red reflector behind, this was usually fixed to the rear mudguard. Batteries could be bought for the lights but they were expensive and didn't last very long especially if they were left in the light during the summer when they were not being used. This resulted in the battery weeping and corroding the inside of the lamp and if left too long the metal rusted through making it impossible to get the battery out. The older people still depended on their carbide lights which worked by putting carbide in a container on the bottom of the lamp and filling another which was above it with water, a tap was turned to allow the water to drip onto the carbide and give off a gas which went up through a burner where a match was held until it lit. Not an easy thing to do if there was a wind blowing and even after it had been alight for some time, a good gust of wind was likely to blow it out as you cycled along. There were dynamos in the shops which operated by running on the side of the tyre and were successful as long as the wheel was turning but as soon as it stopped the light went out and if you slowed down the light dimmed, so as you pedalled along the brightness depended on your speed. In wet weather the dynamo slipped on the wet tyre and gave a light that alternated between bright and dim even when you cycled along at a constant speed.

Many trades supplied bicycles for their employees at work to make deliveries or if they had to travel to do their job. Most shops had their own trade bikes with a basket on the front or bags attached to a carrier over the back wheel while the local window cleaner fitted a carrier for his ladders and bucket on the nearside supported by a third wheel. The red cycles supplied by the Post Office for postmen and the boys delivering telegrams were a familiar sight. The black ones used by railway employees were very similar to the high upright model the local policeman was seen riding, with his black cape folded neatly over the handlebars, as he went about his duty in the villages or on the outskirts of the town. Anyone who could afford a bicycle got one for even if it was only second hand a lot of pleasure could be derived from it. Every child wanted to learn to ride and many taught themselves on their father's bike where they had to sit on the crossbar so they could reach the pedals or put one leg under the crossbar through to the other pedal. It was easier on their mother's cycle as they could just stand on the pedals with no crossbar in the way. There were several older people regularly seen travelling round on three wheeled cycles and of course there were the few who took their cycling seriously and spent their money on racing models in order to train and compete in competitions. Some couples enjoyed touring the countryside on a tandem which was not very practical for everyday use but ideal for two people wishing to get out and about together. The only alternative people had to the bicycle for travelling over short distances or to reach the more remote places in and around the town was to walk.

At the start of the decade everything within the town which

required moving was either done by manpower or horse power and except for the buses and an occasional lorry, that was all the traffic to be seen on the streets of Bungay. People living on the outskirts of the town depended on the oilman calling with his horse drawn cart loaded with all sorts of household goods ranging from kitchenware to all kinds of soaps and polishes. The milkman did his rounds in a milk float while the grocer and greengrocer had ponies pulling purpose built carts with their goods laid out for all to see. Many of the horses got to know the round as well as the man driving them and it was quite usual to see the milk cart moving to the next block of houses while the milkman carried his can and measures directly from door to door so he only had to go to the float when his can required topping up from one of the large urns. Coal carts were a familiar sight as they trundled round the streets or made their way to the goods station to weigh up and bag another load for delivery.

Bags of corn to and from the mill, farms, warehouses and station were carried on larger wagons pulled by much heavier horses and they, like the tumbrels used for general purposes on the farms, were a common sight passing through the town. The local horse dealer in Upper Olland Street had a large black van type of cart, completely closed in with doors at the back which was used by the post office at busy times, such as Christmas, to help with delivery of the parcel post. This must have saved a lot of time and effort for the postmen and it became a familiar sight in the main streets of the town and easy to pick out coming down the road if you were expecting something through the post. Parcels of books and magazines produced at the printers were taken to the goods station for despatch by a carter who used a farm wagon. It was only a very short distance and he had to ensure deliveries were on time as many of these were monthly periodicals for despatch all over the country.

After dark all of these vehicles had to carry lights on both the near and offside and while some had oil many were candlelit. In the town there was some street lighting but on the outskirts and beyond it was dark and as the lights on the cart did little to show the way a great deal must have depended on the horse knowing where he was going. There were advantages with horses at work not least of all the companionship they gave when you worked alone and hours were long. When it was time for a break to sit down and eat the bread and cheese which was carried packed in a lunch tin and take a drink from a bottle of cold tea, the first thing to do was put on the horse's nosebag which was always filled before leaving home in the morning. It was also useful to be able to pop this over his head anytime he had a long wait or something upset him so he became restless.

There were also disadvantages with horses. They required regular feeding with the right food if they were to be worked hard and food was expensive. Some would remain in the stable over the weekend while others would be turned out to grass on Saturday until Monday morning and need no attention during that time whereas if they stayed in they required feeding and watering and the stable cleaned out on all seven days of the week. Some of the horses used on the rounds became well known to the public as they were seen daily pulling their carts from door to door, especially the children who liked to give them a piece of bread or anything they could find for them to eat. These horses could often be found at the weekends with others of different breeds and sizes running together and enjoying their freedom on the common. It was a time consuming job to unharness, feed and bed down a horse after the days work was finished and when the weather was bad they would need a good rub down as well. In winter all of these tasks and a regular grooming had to be carried out in the dim light of a hurricane lamp.

Not all horses were quiet and friendly and some, more difficult than others to handle, were liable  to kick or bite. These sometimes wore blinkers and perhaps a muzzle when they were working in close contact with the public. While it was possible to do something about their aggression there was not much could be done about the mess they made in the streets which they did anywhere at any time no matter if they were moving or standing still and a person could be well splashed just walking on the pavement past a stationary cart if they were not alert to the possibility. Much of the road sweeper's time was spent cleaning up the mess on the roads where the horses had been, although he was helped at times by householders living nearby who rushed out with a bucket and coal shovel to claim the droppings for their garden for it was said to be the best thing ever put around rose trees.

Farmer's were completely dependant on horses for transporting their crops and food as well as working the land and the better off used a pony and trap to take them into town on business or perhaps to meet or catch a train. On these occasions arrangements were made for the horse to be stabled at an inn or public house near to the station. His family had their own small cart to use for shopping or when the wife went calling and if the weather was fine they might use it for a ride around the country on Sunday afternoons or during the school holidays.

As the years passed the volume of motorised traffic increased on the roads but it did so very slowly for although the benefits were very obvious to all and the purchase and maintenance of horses was becoming more and more expensive, few people were in a position to even consider the cost of changing. It was at the end of the decade as the threat of war loomed there seemed to be an almost sudden build up in the number of lorries, cars and motor cycles [often with side cars] on the roads. No doubt they were seen in greater numbers in the larger towns and cities some years earlier because that is where all progress starts. People however had suffered financially for some years with many of them out of work and finding it hard to make ends meet as businesses, including a lot of small farmer's, were made bankrupt and some even evicted from their homes. Now there was an increase in the number of jobs available and although the political outlook was very gloomy people started to have more money in their pockets. Existing roads had to be resurfaced, drained and widened and new ones built to accommodate the greater volume of traffic. New laws were required and soon passed to protect the public and their property. At the same time this happened, with the spread of electricity to most homes, families of all classes took advantage of the chance to buy a modern wireless as they became affordable and readily available. Consequently, what can only be described as a giant step forward was taken by society.

THE COMMON BAILIFF ON A VISIT TO WHARTON STREET

THE RAILWAY STATION AND BRIDGE LEADING TO THE COMMON

# CHAPTER 5.

## SERVICES.

The elected Urban District Council was responsible for the upkeep of the town's roads and all public works which included water and sewerage, street lighting and maintaining a fire service. The feoffees, some of who were life members while others were nominated by the council to fill vacancies as they occurred, assisted the Town Reeve in his work to support the old and underprivileged and served for a period of four years. This Trust was financed by the town's purse and voluntary contributions and it was they who were responsible for the almshouses. Some were very old and it was under the Town Reeve's direction a row of these in Wharton Street were demolished in 1930 clearing the site for a new fire station which they built. The occupants were rehoused in larger and more modern council houses and when the area was cleared and the station completed space remained for two new houses. Some years later the fire station was purchased by the Urban District Council, who took over the funding of the fire brigade.

In the event of a fire the police summoned the firemen by letting off one or two rockets, depending if the fire was in or out of the vicinity of the town and this would bring, not only the firemen but many of the local residents running out excitedly to find where the fire was and see how long it took the engine to get away. Although they were part time volunteers and came from all walks of life as soon as they heard the 'bang' of the rocket they moved as one with a single objective in their minds. There were builders, carpenters and men from all trades dedicated enough to give up their time at a moments notice no matter where they were or what they were doing. A small crowd quickly formed around the station on their return to hear their news and watch them as they hung their hoses to dry and made ready for their next call. They trained and practiced regularly and most men who joined the brigade seemed to stay in it for quite a long time.

It was an organisation always looked upon with great pride and gratification by the population of Bungay. For the younger generation there was the attraction of the dark blue uniform they wore with shining brass buttons, a hatchet hung on a wide leather belt which was secured round the waist by a large buckle at the front and a gleaming helmet to add to the excitement as they watched the engine go off down the road with it's bell clanging to warn everyone of it's approach, the men sat in a row on either side back to back with some still donning and adjusting their uniforms as it sped them away to deal with any emergency.

The postal service was as good as any in the world and probably the cheapest, a letter still only required a penny stamp and delivery could be depended on. Credit for this was due to the organisational skills of the management and the co-operation they received from the railways without who's help the royal mail would have come to a standstill. In the guard's van of most passenger trains the familiar bags, tied and labelled, were laid out in piles ready to be unloaded as the train stopped at each scheduled station on it's journey. Every night the mail trains travelled at high speeds in every direction all over the country with the letters and parcels being sorted as they went. Letters reached every single town and village on the mainland, no matter how small, within a couple of days through the railway network which adhered to strict timetables to connect with these trains. There was a method for dropping off mail destined for places where they did not stop which involved the bags being hung out at the side of the carriage and caught in a contraption rigged alongside the track as the train sped through.

Making two deliveries a day the postman was a well known and familiar figure in his blue uniform with a red trim and  peaked cap. With his large bag slung over his shoulder and carried in front of him across his stomach he went from house to house flicking through a bundle of letters taken from his bag to pick out the ones he wanted as he approached each letter box. For his rounds on the outskirts of the town he used an upright red cycle with his bag strapped to a carrier on the front. Red pillar-boxes were conveniently placed around the town and villages for letters for despatch and these were emptied two or three times a day. Parcels which were too big for the postman to carry in his bag were delivered once a day on a red two wheeled barrow like those used to collect the mail bags from the railway station.

Urgent communications were despatched by telegram and preprinted forms were obtained at the post office, filled in and handed over the counter where a charge was made relating to the number of words to be sent. The message was then phoned or telegraphed through to the post office nearest to it's destination and then delivered by hand. This was a well used service and the messenger was as familiar a sight as the postman in his blue uniform with a round pill box shaped hat secured by a stay under his chin, hurrying along on his red bicycle with a telegram tucked safely in the leather pouch worn on his belt. Although not always the bearer of bad news unexpected telegrams were always received with some apprehension probably because they were strongly associated with the messages received by the families of servicemen killed or missing during the First World War. They were still delivered in the same coloured envelopes with the printed message pasted to the form.

Another service offered by the post office was their savings bank which was widely used by ordinary people, especially those looking for a safe place to save the odd shilling or two for themselves or their children. Anything in the children's book could not be withdrawn until the child reached the age of seven and withdrawal on demand for everyone was limited to three pounds in any one day. The banks offered no service at all to ordinary working people who really had no use for them anyway as their wages were paid in cash each week and paying for everything as it was bought, they were fortunate if they had sufficient funds to meet their needs until the next pay-day. If it was necessary to send money by post, postal orders were available for a small fee from the Post Office and these could be for any amount as stamps were stuck on as necessary to make them up to the value required. A person in receipt of one, only had to sign it before cashing it at any post office. Whereas anyone having a banker's cheque made out to them would not be able to change it themselves but would have to ask a shopkeeper or someone who used a bank to pass it through their account.

The growth in popularity of the football pools resulted in more people requiring the postal order service and at the same time the mail order clubs were being brought to the notice of the public and more widely used. These were operated by men calling at houses with catalogues full of all kinds of goods for which they took the order and arranged for payment to be made by regular weekly or monthly installments. In some cases they called to collect the money when it was due but as business grew and because they were working on a commission basis and needed the time to look for new customers, it was not long before arrangements were made for the money to be sent and the agent would only call again just before the debt was settled to try to make a further sale.

The Urban District Council had both permanent and casual workers and still called on local tradesmen to undertake many tasks. The town's engineer was responsible for the water supply and sewerage as well as many other duties. The main pump on the common had to be maintained and the demand for water increased as more houses had indoor taps and water lavatories installed. Consequently it was necessary for the sewerage facilities to keep pace while at the same time those less fortunate who still awaited modernisation had to be catered for. So it was those men employed during the day on the dustcart doing their rounds of the town emptying dustbins and clearing away rubbish who were called on to work through the night doing the rounds again but this time on the nightcart emptying the buckets from the outside lavatories which were often at the end of the yard or garden. In some areas these men were given an allowance of ten cigarettes a night.

Road sweepers had their regular rounds covering all the streets and roads in the town. They were kept busy, for although there was not so much litter thrown about, there was a constant flow of horse traffic everywhere. The rubbish was most likely to be cigarette ends and empty packets, sweet wrappers, paper bags and perhaps the odd screwed up newspaper which had contained someone's fish and chips the night before. He pushed a two wheeled barrow which housed his broom and shovel as well as the tools he required to clean out the drains which was another of his duties. It was important to clean up the autumn leaves etc. before they went down the drains as all surface drains flowed into ditches before going on into the river and they too had to be kept clear and free flowing.

One man was employed full time at the cemetery cutting the grass and keeping the place tidy. His duties also included digging the graves and taking whatever steps necessary to control the rabbit population. On Sunday mornings, although his day off, he would shave, trim his bushy moustache and stand at the top of the cemetery hill dressed in his Sunday best. With a clean white collar, boots polished, watch chain stretched across a buttoned waistcoat, a trilby hat on his head and with hands behind his back he would nod and greet the people who regularly visited and tended the graves of loved ones at this time. Men took their work very seriously in these days no matter what it entailed and loyalty and dedication was evident even among those doing the most menial jobs. Of course, there was always the possibility of a tip in appreciation of that little extra care and attention shown to particular individuals.

Roadworks always seemed to attract the attention of the public regardless of who was doing it. No matter if it was the gas or water companies laying pipes or just repairs to the surface the work was done by a gang of men with pick axes and shovels. The only mechanical help they got was on the bigger tasks like resurfacing when a steam roller was brought in to flatten it down and that was certain to cause excitement, especially among the younger members of the community who liked to run beside it as it rumbled noisily along the road, it's own particular warm smoky smell mingling with that given off by the hot tar.

When the working day ended the shovels, picks and other tools were all collected up and placed together alongside the watchman's hut next to the lamps he would have already cleaned, filled with oil and trimmed that morning so they were ready to be lit and placed around the working area as soon as it began to get dark. One of the first jobs the watchman did on arrival for work was to light the brazier which was positioned in front of his hut and make sure he had sufficient coke to keep it burning all night. This was going to keep him warm and ensure his kettle was boiling for the frequent brews of tea for himself and any visitors he might have. His hut was usually made by pulling a tarpaulin sheet over a frame leaving the front open so he had a good view of all he had to keep an eye on, it was really just enough to protect him from the wind and rain.

His was a lonely job and as the hours passed there were less and less people to be seen so it is little wonder he welcomed the odd person stopping for a warm around the fire and a chat. Young people often got to know the watchman and liked to huddle in the hut and listen to his stories, sometimes accompanied by the patter of rain on the tarpaulin and the sizzle it made on the fire as well as the occasional whiff of sulphur which seemed to waft into their faces every now and then as they gazed into the flames. This was the kind of work often done by disabled veterans of the

First World War so it is little wonder the children were fascinated by the tales they heard. People like the policeman on his rounds were always pleased to stop and warm themselves round the fire on a cold night .

Water was now being piped to all areas in the town with taps replacing the existing pumps, although many people still had to share a tap with several other families. All new houses could expect water laid on over a shallow sink and a flush toilet which was now being put inside the main building and sometimes upstairs as part of the bathroom suite. The town pump in the Market Place was no longer required and it was decided to do away with this and at the same time replace the lamps on it by a standard with much brighter electric lighting. The Town Reeve proposed to depict the notorious Black Dog of Bungay as a weather vane above the lights and organised a competition among the young people of the town to see who could submit the best drawing of the beast. After careful consideration it was decided to call a draw and use the front and head from one entry and the rear and tail of another and so the Black Dog was designed and presented to the town as a constant reminder of the legend. The installation of the electric lights reduced the duties of the lamplighter who's job it was to light the gas lights in the streets at night then extinguish them at dawn and during the day he would have to clean them and check the mantles ready for another night when he would go out again with the long pole he carried to enable him to reach high enough to turn on the gas and light the mantles.

Having water and electricity readily available was probably one of the biggest revolutions ever to take place in the home and was to make an immense difference, not only to the woman's workload but to the living standards of the whole family. As the decade passed more and more electrically operated labour saving devices came on the market and although most were out of the range of the pockets of ordinary people they had the effect of raising their hopes and expectations.

Once installed the electricity was paid for by putting money in a meter which always seemed to be placed in the most convenient place for the people putting it in but the worst possible place for the householder. They were to be found in such places as the cupboard under the stairs, over the bedroom door at the top of the stairs or in a recess in the bedroom. It was always somewhere dark and inaccessible so when the man called unexpectantly to empty the meter there was a rush to tidy up and move things out of his way or find something for him to stand on. However, this was small price to pay for the benefits derived from the new bright lights and other luxuries that could be looked forward to even if they were out of reach for the time being. One good thing, you only paid for as much power as you could afford. Some of the first meters were operated with pennies but it was not long before they were all changed and required shillings. At the same time there was an arrangement whereby a kind of bonus was given in the form of a rebate if there was more than a certain amount in the meter at the time it was emptied. Electricity was now in direct competition with gas both for heating and lighting and the former quickly proved it was more efficient, easier to operate, cleaner, without smell and above all, much safer. Lighting was everyone's first priority but it was soon followed by an urgent desire to get a quick boiling electric kettle, an iron which stayed at a constant heat and a clean easily controllable cooker.

As more households installed electricity the sale of wirelesses increased and gave a new meaning to communication as many more people could now be reached in their own homes. Radio personalities, like film stars, became well known and soon influenced their fans who were always eager to imitate them and follow their example. Wireless poles appeared in gardens and back yards or even on the rooftop to support the ariel for the longer and higher it was the better the reception, or so it was claimed. Until now, unless a member of the family was able to play a musical instrument and had one, the only music heard in the home would be from a gramophone which was wound up with a handle as each record was put onto the turntable. They often had the sound amplified by a large horn. Only members of the middle classes would have been likely to be able to afford such a gramophone or stretch to the price of instruments like a piano, or violin so, for many people, different styles of music and other forms of entertainment were being brought to them for the first time in their own homes.

Coal was very expensive and many households supplemented it by burning wood which could be bought at the local woodyard or they could collect it themselves, if they had permission, from the woods and countryside. Those living in the vicinity of the gas works could take a barrow or old pram along and purchase a bag of coke which they mixed with coal or wood and was very efficient except for the smell and fumes it gave off.

In the Summer, during hot dry spells the water cart was pulled around the town spraying all the main roads to cool them and keep the dust down, while in the winter when the snow covered the roads the snow plough would be brought out to clear them and men with shovels dug it from the pavements and gutters. During really bad weather when the roads were covered in ice and very slippery the horse pulling the snow plough as well as any other working horses who had to be on the roads, had nails left protruding from their shoes to help them get a grip. Nevertheless they had a job keeping their feet when negotiating hills like Bridge Street in such hazardous conditions and they often had to call for extra help in the form of manpower or horsepower to enable them to reach the Market Place at the top. Of course going down the hill with a heavy load was an even bigger problem as any brakes there might be on the cart or wagon would have little or no effect under these conditions when the locked wheels just slipped pushing the horse before it.

# CHAPTER 6.

## CHILDREN. - AT SCHOOL.

Young children are not often aware of the adverse conditions their parents live under unless there is a sudden change to some everyday happening which has a direct affect on them and consequently, those born and brought up during an economic recession, not knowing anything different, accept and make the most of things as they are. It is as they get older and start looking at people and circumstances outside their own family circle they realise others are sometimes better or worse off than themselves and such a realisation can easily affect their behaviour which in turn upsets the harmony of every day life in the family.

Before starting school they were constantly under the watchful eye of their mother, who, with the help of the rest of the family, was always near at hand to comfort and respond to any one of the numerous demands made by very small children and during their first five years they rarely left her side. When they did they were likely to be cared for by another member of the family especially when there were brothers and sisters. Babies were proudly paraded in their prams or pushchairs to be shown off to friends and neighbours and mothers would meet in the afternoons to exchange views and compare the qualities and progress of their offspring. Until they were old enough to go to school this was likely to be the only contact  young children had with others outside the family.

Starting school at the age of five was something of a shock to them, for the first time they were on their own with no mother to turn to when things were not quite right. The teachers employed for the infants were very good at their job and seemed to be the most loyal and long serving of all teachers. They often found they had the children of former pupils in their class and it was unusual if it took them more than a couple of days to win the confidence of even the most reserved child. It was at this point in the child's life, as they got to know and associate with other youngsters, they started to compare what they had with what those around them appeared to have. Unfortunately, things were not always as they seemed through the eyes of a young child and very often those that looked privileged to their fellows at school and acted the part, would be seen in a much different way after a visit to their home. Many of the poorer people were very proud and made a great effort to hide their poverty. Others, especially those with larger families, had little choice and it would have been futile to even attempt to conceal anything for their social standing was usually quite obvious from the way their children were clothed and presented at school.

Children soon settled down to school life and made friends. Sometimes just two children together while others congregated in groups from which natural leaders soon emerged, unfortunately they were not always the ones the teachers or parents would have chosen. Sometimes, to boost their own ego or simply through envy, young people are cruel and unfeeling towards each other and because of the big difference in the living standards of families many youngsters from the less privileged homes were soon targets for bullying and abuse by those who were better off. A certain amount of jealousy was inevitable when some children attended school well dressed with food and fruit of some kind for their lunch while others wearing well worn and ill fitting second hand clothes would expect and get nothing to eat between breakfast and whatever they might have when they went home for dinner. For those who could afford it, some of the schools supplied a bottle of milk, which was one third of a pint and cost a halfpenny a day.

Those from similar backgrounds tended to stick together both in and outside the classroom. Had this been a straightforward case of those that have and those that have not in equal numbers, it would have been easy to deal with but no two families were the same. Even those with similar incomes had different values and spent their money according to their priorities so no two children could possibly have the same outlook or expectations. In every yearly intake of pupils there was an unequal mixture of backgrounds as well as social and moral standards.

Except for those attending private preparatory schools, all children started at the Council School or Roman Catholic school at the age of five where they stayed until they were eleven when the more advanced who passed the Scholarship exam had an opportunity to move to a grammar school. In those early years teachers concentrated on basic subjects with emphasis on reading, writing and arithmetic. Classes were overcrowded and with only their own assessment of a child's ability to guide them the teacher's job was a very important and difficult one. The lessons were set to the standard of the brightest in the class which resulted in the slower and more backward pupils, not only being left behind, but dropping further back each year. There was little the teachers could do about it and after failing the Scholarship exam children often lost all interest in education and a few of the more irresponsible ones frequently played truant. Such an offence would be punished by caning, after a reprimand, by the headmaster who would then advise the parents. They in turn might administer their own punishment or not bother. It was not unknown among the poorer families for a father to keep his son away from school to assist him with some task especially when the boy had reached the age of thirteen and seemed to be achieving nothing in the classroom, waiting only to reach the age of fourteen when he could leave if he had a job to go to. If no work was available pupils remained at school until they were fifteen.

Although most parents were extremely interested in their children's progress at school they had little or no involvement at all in school matters. The infants had concerts, carol services and plays at certain times of the year to which they were invited and all were welcome to the annual school Sports Day when everyone at the school was expected to do something to help. Meetings with the teachers however were confined mainly to those occasions when complaints or questions of discipline required discussion.

No uniform or compulsory dress was worn by the pupils at these schools and many boys turned up in ill fitting and torn trousers which should have been worn just above the knee but were often baggy and came down over the knees or were very tight and short so they easily split. They were generally held up by braces over a shirt which was buttoned at the neck with slits either side at the bottom giving a generous long tail to tuck between the legs [not many boys from the poorer families had underclothes to wear]. In colder weather this was covered with a jersey which was pulled over the head and buttoned up to a small collar at the neck. Those who had them wore black laced up ankle boots over long socks with a pattern around a turned over top. The boots concealed any holes in the heels of the socks which were often seen crumpled down around the ankles but holes in the soles or toes of the boots themselves and string which often replaced laces were clearly visible.

Girls always managed to look much cleaner and tidier than the boys even though they too often had to make do with second hand and shabby clothing. There were some families who were able to afford to dress their children well and they did and one thing they didn't have to worry too much about was following fashion because for most children at this time it wasn't considered. In such hard times people dressed their children in the best they could with priority given to warmth and wear rather than appearance.

As always, some teachers were much stricter than others and more ready to deal out punishment, each having their own preference as to what it should be. Minor offences were dealt with immediately by reprimand, extra work [like lines], stopping behind after school finished for the day, standing in front of the class or in a corner, being sent out of the classroom or hit on the hand with a ruler. For anything more serious the pupil was sent to the Headmaster who had more serious options such as the cane and expulsion. Of course there were many cases when a book, a piece of chalk or other object was thrown across the classroom at a child who was inattentive.

These schools had very little organised sport other than games supervised by the teachers in the playground or an occasional visit to the playing field on the Honeypot Meadow and there was very little equipment provided for these activities. The boys played football and cricket improvising by using their coats, jerseys or almost any object they could lay their hands on to serve as goal posts and while wickets were easily chalked on a suitable wall for the batting end, an item of clothing was likely to be used to mark the position of the bowler's end.

At one time some of the older girls played hockey but as they had to provide their own sticks many could only watch. Younger pupils spent their playtime running after one another or huddled in small groups dotted around the playground telling stories, sharing secrets or perhaps showing off a favourite toy. Some girls got a lot of pleasure as well as exercise by skipping and became quite expert doing varied steps to the chanting of well known verses by their companions who turned the rope for them.

Chalk which was often often brought to school in large lumps was a valuable commodity in the playground where it was used to mark boundaries for many of the games and was essential when drawing the squares for the ever popular hop scotch which was enjoyed by both boys and girls. Unfortunately there was always someone who preferred to use the chalk to deface walls to pass an anonymous derogatory message expressing their feelings and these were usually directed at a teacher or another pupil. This resulted in chalk being banned from time to time and any child caught with a piece was punished but somehow they still managed to mark out the playground when they wanted to play. At one time a pitch was officially marked out for netball and portable nets, stored in an outhouse, were brought out when games were organised by the teachers. This was acceptable to most children as it was played in school hours and even when they were watching and awaiting their turn to play it was a welcome break from lessons and sitting in a stuffy classroom.

During the Summer months classes of older pupils were taken down to the river at the Staithe for swimming lessons and a board was fixed just above the water on the quay at the shallow end to make it easier for the children to get in and out. The non swimmers would wear an inflated lifebuoy round their waist to which the instructor attached a line so he was able to hold them up while he walked along the board and told them what to do. The weather and the water were not often warm enough for this kind of coaching to be effective but no doubt the children were happy to take advantage of the opportunity to get outside and away from school for an hour.

Children attending the grammar schools found things much different. The large majority were from families who could afford to pay the fees with the remainder made up of those passing the Scholarship. Girls who passed had to attend Sir John Lemon School at Beccles as there was nowhere for them to go in Bungay. St Mary's School for girls accepted only paying pupils who were able to sit for the School Certificate when they were sixteen. It was also a preparatory school for boys up to the age of ten.

Bungay Grammar School catered for boys only and their curriculum, which was quite extensive, included Mathematics, English [language and literature], Geography, History, Languages [French and Latin], Sciences, Religious Instruction, Current Affairs, Art and Woodwork. Originally boys could start at the age of ten from a preparatory school but in the mid 1930's the second form was abolished and all had to start in the third form at the age of eleven.

Each subject was taught by the appropriate master in his own room, so at the end of each lesson all pupils moved from one classroom to another. There were groups of lockers built into the wall all down one side of the main corridor and one was allocated to each boy, with a key, when he started school and this was where he was expected to keep his books etc. so they could be easily changed between lessons. The partitions between the three centre classrooms folded back to make one large hall where every morning the whole school assembled for prayers. Before the prayers actually started the Headmaster would accept and read the letters from parents handed in by those who had not attended the day before giving the reason for their absence and this was the time he would make any special announcement he had for the whole school.

While the pupils awaited the arrival of the teachers who preceded the Headmaster into the hall, absolute silence had to be observed by everyone, to enforce this the prefects moved among the boys, often with a large book borrowed from the library ready to come down on the head of anyone who dared to speak or find something to giggle about. Prefects were able to give various kinds of punishment at their discretion when they caught someone doing wrong, like running in the corridor or being discourteous toward a senior. This could range from a two to four page essay or lines to be finished and handed in the next day, to ten or more cubes. For these the boy was given a number in the the hundreds which was multiplied by itself, then the answer by the same number again, the next number was treated the same way and the next and so on until the total number of cubes which had been given were completed.

The first shock for all new pupils was the realisation they had spent the previous year as the oldest and most senior in the school where they had a hand in all activities and they now found themselves to be the youngest, in the bottom class and having to do exactly what they were told by everybody. For the scholarship boys it was worse as a good deal of snobbery existed and the strict discipline was often in the hands of the prefects who were sixth formers staying on, having got their School Certificate, to take the Higher before going on to Cambridge University. Boys and girls attending Sir John Lemon School at Beccles who passed their exams went on to Oxford University.

All the parents of the new pupils were notified well before the term started of the school's rules which were to be strictly adhered to and one of the first things to be sorted out was the uniform which had to be purchased from Wightman's in St Mary's Street. The cap with badge and tie were compulsory and had to be worn always. It was expected that pupils would attend dressed in grey shirt and trousers, black shoes and for those under fourteen years of age wearing short trousers, grey school socks with black and white tops. A black school blazer bearing the school badge on the pocket was most desirable and a satchel to carry the books required for homework was essential. Most started the first day dressed in the full uniform which was not so much of a problem for the better off but even with the allowance made to the poorer scholarship pupils it was a struggle to keep up. From the first day there was ongoing expenses, sports attire was needed from the start and each of the three terms in turn called for hockey stick, football boots then cricket boots or shoes and later full whites if selected for a house or school team.

All of the sports equipment was supplied and with a sports master attending on two days of the week a great emphasis was put on all sporting activities. Only on medical grounds could anyone be excused physical training which took place outside on the playing field unless the weather was really bad. The kit worn for this was sports vest and shorts with nothing allowed under them and white gym shoes. Each class had one or two half hour sessions each week and on days when the sports master was not in attendance it was taken by one of the other teachers. All kinds of gymnastics were performed as well as events like the javelin, throwing a cricket ball, hurdles, high and long jumps and there was an annual inter house boxing tournament at all weights. When the class was spread out doing exercises taking instruction from the front, it was usual for one of the prefects to walk among them to ensure they put every ounce of energy into their efforts and if he thought they were not, he sometimes carried a pair of kid gloves with which he administered a sharp slap on a leg or bent over backside to make them try harder.

Every boy had to pay a sports subscription of a minimum of one shilling each term. They were expected to pay more and were put under pressure to do so. The responsibility for collecting this was given to the captain of each house who naturally wanted his house to make a bigger contribution than any of the others and made a determined effort to see that it did. This sometimes made life very difficult for scholarship boys whose parents could not afford to give them more.

Competitions between the houses were in progress throughout every term and some of these, like track events, culminated on the annual Sports Day when all parents and many other VIP's were invited and refreshments were provided for the guests between events. All entrants represented their house and points were awarded to all the winners and runners up of each event. These were added up and the afternoon would end with the presentation of a cup by the Guest of Honour to the captain of the winning house. There were cups to be won and awarded for every sport right through the year and all were very competitively fought for.

Mostly pupils took part in sport after school was finished in the afternoon although those who had long distances to travel home and brought a packed dinner could indulge themselves on the playing field for an hour while others went home for their meal. If the weather was bad there were table tennis tables in the centre classroom and bats and balls were held in the common room by the duty master. Some boys who lived locally would rush back as soon as they had eaten to join in with them. Those staying had to eat their food in the cloakroom unless the weather was warm enough to sit outside. There were quite a lot of pupils attending from places as far apart as Southwold, Poringland and Pulham Market who travelled in by bus or train while those from further afield boarded at either Emmanual or Dunelm House.

The dinner hour could be usefully spent catching up on homework and the new library which was built in the mid 1930's was an ideal place to go and sit to do it for there was no noise other than the wireless which was played quietly at all times and there were always ample seats and tables available.

Homework was something else the new pupils soon got used to. Normally there would be three subjects set to take approximately half an hour each every night but it was unlikely that any but the brightest could do them conscientiously in that time and there was always a certain few who never seemed to try but waited until morning when they would attempt to engage the assistance of a colleague who had completed his or failing that, try to frighten a smaller boy into releasing his books long enough for them to be able to make some showing in their own before classes started.

As with other schools the Grammar School was very advantageous for the more intelligent and talented pupils while others who were average or below struggled on as well as they were able. Anyone with outstanding ability in the classroom or on the playing field was helped and nurtured and given every opportunity as were most of those from upper middle class families. There was however a big plus for all who attended as great emphasis was put on the way boys conducted themselves and the good manners and respect they showed toward their elders. At all times teachers were addressed as 'sir' and no question was considered without a 'please' and the answer always acknowledged with a 'thank you'. Opening and holding doors for teachers and adults, raising their hat and moving out of the way to pass on the outside of the pavement when they met in the street soon became an automatic action. The surprising thing was that after performing a courteous act most found they felt an unaccountable warm feeling of satisfaction. The efforts made to encourage local boys to drop their accent and speak properly together with regular contact and speaking and working with boys from other areas did a great deal to improve their elocution. All of this meant that even if a boy left the school at sixteen without reaching the required academic standard he had at least built a character which gave him  strength to meet any challenge he had to face in the future with confidence.

One of the most important days for the school was the annual Speech Day, the culmination of the academic and the sports year when all interested parents attended to hear the Headmaster's report and forecast for the next twelve months. House captains were called up to receive the appropriate cups or shields won by the members of their house but for many of the visitors the highlight of the afternoon was hearing of the achievements of individuals in various subjects as they were summoned in turn to receive their prize which was usually a book relating to the field they excelled in.

No matter which school they attended all children faced the problem of finding suitable employment when their education was completed. It was difficult enough to find a job of any kind and anyone able to enter a trade or profession of their choice considered themselves very fortunate. This did not apply to the upper class who attended private schools, usually as boarders, where the name of the school together with their family background almost guaranteed their position in society. Even with a shortfall in academic standards it was generally assumed, if it came to the worst, there was still a choice between the army, the church or politics where the family name and standing were the only qualifications requiring close scrutiny.

Still, it was not as easy for them as it had been in years gone by when the Empire absorbed large numbers of young men with such social standing through the Foreign Office and filling the many and varied posts within the companies operating abroad. Many of the larger and smaller businesses in this country were just beginning to question the wisdom of what was the normal practice of allowing a son, with or without the necessary qualification, to automatically follow in his father's footsteps in the family business and taking precedence over others who might be better qualified. With money short and order books virtually empty those customers remaining, finding they had a wide choice and seriously considering their own stability, were starting to look to those firms who showed the most initiative and efficiency and this had to originate in the Board Room. So the pressure was already being felt by some of the youngsters who had hitherto enjoyed a privileged childhood.

BUNGAY GRAMMAR SCHOOL

CHAPTER 7.


CHILDREN - AT LEISURE.


School children had quite a lot of time to themselves and although it is easy to remember how it was spent in the Summer when the weather was nice, it is difficult to recall much of what was done when it was wet and cold, perhaps because there was very little for anyone to do. With large families accommodated in small houses children were generally encouraged by their parents to play outside and until they were considered old enough to go off on their own they were instructed to stay close to home with the familiar words 'don't you go away!' uttered to them as they went out, this meant they were to stay in their own back yard or go onto the road where they would be within earshot if they were called.

Once they had chosen their companions and decided what they wanted to do, the older children had a wide choice of places where they could go and play. One of the biggest attractions for any child, no matter what age they were or what time of the year it might be, was the river and this was the one place in particular parents forbade any of their children to go without supervision unless they happened to be very strong swimmers. There had been a number of tragic accidents in the past which were often spoken about to remind everyone of the dangers. All around were lots of open spaces where they could play safely and in the town itself they had the Honeypot Meadow and Castle Hills as well as other areas but the roads often proved to be the most popular place to get together and enjoy various pastimes and games.

Other than in the main streets there was not much danger to the children as they bowled their hoops and spun their tops which were often decorated with coloured chalks or had pieces of silver paper pasted on them to create attractive patterns as they whirled around. These were made of wood with a metal stud in the bottom on which it spun and grooves all around the middle where the string of a whip was twisted to start it spinning, once going it was hit with the whip and propelled down the road, then as it slowed down it was hit again to keep it spinning. The only danger from these tops was, if the string of the whip got caught around it when it was being hit, it was likely to fly into the air and possibly strike someone or perhaps break a window. In the event of the stud coming out a friendly shoemaker would be visited in the hope he could be talked into putting a new one in.

Tops and hoops were enjoyed by both boys and girls and while girls also enjoyed hop scotch, skipping and playing with their dolls, the boys passed their time away crouched down on the pavement playing five stones, marbles or cigarette cards [better known as 'fag cards']. Sets of cards covering a wide range of subjects were issued by all the cigarette manufacturers and a card was inserted in every packet of cigarettes sold. Books to collect these in were usually given away free and had spaces for three or four cards on a page with four small slits for each into which the corners were tucked to hold them in. The description which appeared on the back of the card was repeated underneath or sometimes at the side. Later some of the cards were issued with adhesive backs so they could be moistened and stuck in but these were not so well liked as they tended to be thinner and did not stand up so well  to the game of 'flickums' which was played against a wall or fence, preferably in a corner, with just two people who stood with their toe behind a selected line and flicked a card in turn, the first one to cover any part of another card won all those on the ground. There were always some cards in each set very difficult to get while others were easy and for a time, until everyone wanted the same ones to complete a set, the spares were held as 'swops' after which they were used to play with. For those interested in the subjects represented these were educational as well as of general interest. There were sets of railway engines, birds, wild animals, kings and queens of England, film stars, racehorses and almost every other subject of public interest. Men calling at one of the sweet shops or tobacconists on their way to or from work for their cigarettes were regularly approached by boys cadging the card.

In all walks of life there are people who like to collect things and children at this time were no different although for most, it had to be something which did not have to be paid for. Stamp collections were started by many but few continued with it after they had stuck the more common ones in a beginner's album which they were most likely to have been given as a birthday or christmas present. One popular item easy to collect was matchbox tops. The label had to be carefully peeled or steamed off the box and stuck into a book. Everyone used matches and many companies used the labels on the boxes to promote themselves and issued their own brands for sale or some, like the brewers, gave them away. Certain sweets and bubblegum were issued with the name of a celebrity printed on each wrapper and a gift could be claimed in exchange for a complete set. Needless to say there was always one name that every collector finally wanted and never got. A brand of chewing gum did a promotion using the names of famous boxers and offered a pair of boxing gloves to anyone who sent them the full set of wrappers. It seemed everybody in Bungay was able to buy or swop every one except Gene Tunney and no one was ever known to claim the prize.

In the Spring some boys went bird nesting, firstly to find the nests and then to take an egg either for their collection or, if they already had one of that kind, to swop for one they hadn't got. Most got a lot of pleasure doing this and watching the birds and they took great care not to scare them from their nest and generally abided by their own unwritten rules and would not take an egg unless there were more than two, although everyone could not be trusted to stick to this self imposed code. A pin or sharp object was used to pierce a hole at the top and bottom of the egg. By placing the mouth against the hole at the top the contents could be blown out of the shell. Unfortunately this called for a certain amount of skill and resulted in many shells being broken in the process, which would then sometimes create an irresistible urge to return to the nest for another.

Many different ball games were played by boys and girls. Chalk was used to mark a line on the road to represent a net for a game of tennis. Often a couple of old rackets with broken strings or which had warped, as they did if they were not kept in a press at all times when they were not being used, could be found or borrowed. If not, a piece of wood served as a bat and a jersey or cap was put down to mark the corners for rounders. A ball of any kind and size would do for a game of football. If there were only a few playing they made do with one goal, preferably in front of a solid wall of some sort, with a lamp post, dustbin or any other object handy serving as goalposts. Without a ball boys kicked almost anything around and one thing always in demand from the butcher was a pig's bladder which blown up and tied would stand quite a lot of rough treatment before it burst. Hoardings, like those built in front of the unused small mill in Staithe Road were ideal for marking out a goal or in summer, wickets for a game of cricket. The road was very wide at this point and play would not be interrupted by anything other than pedestrians, cyclists or an odd wagon going to or coming from the mill at the Staithe.

As they got older children ventured further from home and all did quite a lot of walking as they developed favourite places to play. There were woods where they could climb trees and Bath hills where they showed off their prowess climbing up the hill situated on the riverside known as 'Target', this was looked on as a challenge by both young and old in the town. It was on jaunts such as these at certain times of the year when they occupied themselves collecting seasonal produce from the countryside for their amusement. Conkers were collected and removed from their prickly cases then, after making a hole through them with something like a steel meat skewer they were threaded onto string ready to compete against all comers in a conker fight. Two competitors took turns hitting their opponents conker until one was smashed off it's string. For two or three weeks everyone challenged the champions and tried to find new ways of making their conker more durable than any they might challenge. Many tricks were tried like baking them in the oven or soaking them in vinegar or other solutions but nothing really made them any better for the task and if it was found the conker had been treated in some way the contender was disqualified.

Pop guns were always popular among young boys who kept their eyes open as they roamed around for a suitable elder tree. A saw had to be borrowed to cut a straight length of stout wood about a foot long, then a thin but strong piece of steel [like a spoke from a bicycle wheel] was used to push the pith from the centre of it leaving a clean hole right through. Another piece of wood a few inches longer and with about the same circumference as the elder was cut to fit tightly into the hole through the centre leaving one end to the full size to serve as a handle. Acorns were collected for ammunition, they were peeled and halved [often with the teeth] and using the handle, one half was hammered as tightly as possible into the holes at each end. The handle was then placed against the stomach and forced into one end of the hole with the gun held firmly in both hands, then, with a sharp pull down the half acorn at the other end was forced out of the gun with a loud pop. If there were no acorns available for ammunition newspaper soaked or chewed up was a good substitute but did not travel quite so far.

One thing always in children's thoughts was their stomach and as the seasons passed the countryside produced many things which were edible and readily available to youngsters. Chestnuts, hazelnuts and even the nuts from the beech trees were collected. Blackberries were good to eat but if you knew someone who wanted them, they could be sold for a penny or two and so well worth collecting to take home. There was always one boy or girl willing to taste any berry or leaf which were said to be edible but most stuck to the things they knew were good, like fruit and nuts or even a turnip found growing on the side of a field. Everyone liked to pick wild flowers and children would walk miles to gather a bunch of snowdrops, violets, primroses or cowslips depending on the time of year, to take home for their mother or grandmother.

When rambling, boys liked to carry a stick selected from the hedgerow which was useful for holding aside brambles and beating down nettles. There was also a chance of coming across an adder [better known as a viper], the only poisonous snake to be found in East Anglia. The adder population was increasing in numbers rapidly enough for notices to be posted warning people of their presence and informing them that if they saw one they had a duty to kill it. Needless to say many were unable to tell an adder from a grass snake and even those that could often chose to hurry away in the opposite direction if they saw anything that resembled one.

All boys were proud to own and carry a knife of some kind and found many uses for it from cutting a stick to carving initials on a tree. They were always on the lookout for a good Y-shaped stick suitable for a catapult which they could cut and keep while they set about getting the elastic and tying the ends to each side of fork with a piece of leather to hold the missile secured in the centre. Square elastic was sold in the shops especially for the purpose but it was expensive and most youngsters made do with any kind they could find and put something like the tongue from an old shoe in the middle. Complete ready-made catapults were available from hardware stores with metal handles but only adults were able to afford them and only people like gamekeepers or poachers were likely to have any real use for them and buy them. With practice and carefully selected stones they proved to be a very lethal weapon, which is why boys who had them kept them out of sight for fear they would be confiscated by parents, teachers or the local policeman. They were dangerous in the hands of youngsters and responsible for many minor accidents as well as a lot of broken windows.

Stores and shops received much of their stock in wooden boxes or crates, many of which were non-returnable and eagerly sought after to be put to many uses. The best known and one of the strongest was the tea chest which was quite large, made of plywood and would usually cost a few pence. There were others in all shapes and sizes which the older children were keen to take off their hands to make into things like a locker for their pet rabbit or a cage for their white mice. Barrows and go-carts were popular but difficult to construct without adult help but there were still quite a few of them to be seen, large and small, some sophisticated with a steering wheel and brake and others no more than a box on four wheels steered with the feet. There was one thing they all had in common, they could only go as fast as the boy who was pushing them could run, that is until they came to a hill when their speed increased rapidly and the brake, which was usually no more than a piece of wood bolted to the side and held onto the wheel, did little to check it. There is no doubt the children had great fun in these contraptions but they were a menace to everyone when they were raced on the roads and pavements.

Discipline for youngsters in the home was strict and probably even more so in larger families where they quickly learned to do as they were told without question or to accept punishment. If they ran a little wild when away from their home and school they knew the risk and the likely consequences if they were caught. For some this added to the excitement and although any punishment was painful at the time, it was quick and soon forgotten. In most households there was a set time for meals, for going to bed and for getting up and regular duties were allocated to all members of the family and generally these were adhered to. There are times however when, with or without reason, children are naughty. There was a strong belief in the saying 'spare the rod and spoil the child' and many parents administered physical punishment with their hands while a few went further and used a belt or stick. Except in the more extreme cases it is debatable if this had any lasting effect on the children who seemed to grow up with just as much affection for their parents and no ill feeling toward society.

Money was something youngsters saw very little of and even a few pence pocket money each week could only be dreamed of by many of the children who were lucky to get a penny or perhaps only a halfpenny to take to one of the sweet shops where they had a large selection of confectionery to choose from. One penny could buy two ounces of most of the unwrapped sweets while a farthing was enough for some single items like chews, a liquorice pipe or a toffee shoelace. There were all sorts of sweets in jars and boxes, bars of nougat, chocolate, coconut ice, toffee, sticks of liquorice, chewing and bubble gum, tiger nuts, lotus beans, bull's eyes, aniseed balls, chocolate chewing nuts, wine gums, lollypops and large round sweets [called 'gob stoppers'] which changed colour as they were eaten. One of these could be concealed in the corner of a handkerchief and then sucked during lessons in school while pretending to wipe your nose. Then there were toffee apples, sherbet fountains, packets of crisps and lots more to choose from.

Older children were always looking for chances to earn a copper or two and each season offered different opportunities. The best time was the summer during the school holidays when there was a demand for ball boys at the bowls club, tennis tournaments and if you were big and strong enough they sometimes needed caddies on the golf course. Strawberries were the first fruit ready for picking and children could accompany their mothers when they were employed to do this. These were followed by other fruit through the summer until it was time for the back breaking task in the potato fields. This work was too heavy for children on their own but they still helped to pick the potatoes up and fill the basket or sack as it was moved along by their mother. Girls as well as boys often earned a penny or two running errands for friends and neighbours or the older folk who could not get out to the shops themselves. The most frequent source of pocket money for many youngsters was their grandparents where they were usually given something when they called whether they earned it or not.

Rabbits were another source of income for the young and at harvest time, if you had permission, a good heavy stick and the ability to use it was all that was required to catch the rabbits as they ran out when the corn was being cut. The farmer cut round the outside of the field first working towards the centre and as he did so the rabbits moved to the middle in an attempt to get out of the way with only the odd one or two making a run for it. When only a small piece in the centre remained to be cut everyone formed a circle round it and moved in ready for the moment when, with no cover left, the rabbits remaining had to make a bolt for safety. With guns and dogs as well as sticks to get past their chance of survival was not very good. The spoils of the day were usually shared and there was a ready market for any that were surplus to their own needs. If a boy was really enterprising, having sold the rabbit for a few pence, he would offer to skin it as a favour and then take the skin to a dealer in Upper Olland Street who would buy it from him and hang it in the roof of his shed with lots of others he had already bought. The price paid depended on size, quality and the market and could be as little as two or as much as ten pence.

Everyone had fires to light and required kindling which had to be found or bought and this created another opportunity for those willing to go round the shops and collect old wooden boxes which were to be thrown out, chop them up and tie them in small bundles. A home made barrow, even if it was only a box on an old pair of pram wheels with two handles nailed on, was then needed to cart it from house to house and sell it. After doing this for a while it was possible for a boy to build up a round with customers who depended on a regular call.

Choir boys received a payment every quarter of a sum between one and sixpence and three shillings depending on their seniority, attendance and quality of voice. This seemed like a small fortune to some but unless pleasure was derived from the duties entailed three months was a long time to wait for the money. However there were other perks for them. They were allowed to go on the christmas outing to Norwich which was attended by all members of the choir and the vicar sometimes held a christmas party for them at the vicarage.

All children who attended sunday school were able to go on an outing to the seaside which was organised during the Summer holidays when they all went to Lowestoft for the day. Mothers would see their children off on a special train from the station in the morning making sure they had a packed lunch and impressing on then that the food was not to be eaten until the teacher told them to. On arrival they made straight for the beach where they played and paddled all of the morning until they were called to sit in a semi circle around their teacher and eat their food. Next there was a trip to the shops, particularly Woolworths where tall girls with painted red lips and cheeks served behind long counters filled with every kind of gift they could ever think of to take home for their mothers and nothing cost more than sixpence. Everyone saved enough to buy an ice cream as they left for they had a taste to be remembered and an association with the warm pleasant smell of the store. Shopping completed they all trooped to a church hall where tables covered with white cloths were laid with a place for everyone to sit and gorge the sandwiches, jellies, cakes and lemonade set before them. Then it was time for the train home and reunion with their parents who would be waiting at the station to hear a joyful account of the day's events. This outing was the highlight of the summer for many youngsters and much appreciated by all.

The cinema had a big influence on the young as well as the old and no matter how good or bad the weather might be the matinee on Saturday afternoons at the New Theatre was always popular and well attended and although there was no such thing as a queue, children were to be seen crowding around the ticket office a good half hour before the doors opened. Admission was threepence and for that they saw a full feature and supporting film as well as a cartoon and of course a serial which went on each week. Talking pictures had arrived and the manager spent much of his time walking up and down the aisles trying to quieten the youngsters who, in their excitement, shouted warnings and advice to their heroes. The serials, with each weekly episode finishing at a point of high drama, were a big encouragement for the audience to return the following week. No matter if the hero was a cowboy, deep sea diver, hunter or anything else the whole episode would be re-enacted by children in scores of back yards or any suitable location many times during the week.

While the musicals and high society films captured the imagination of the older members of the population, it was the cowboys, gangsters, war and adventure pictures as well as the characters in them the youngsters enjoyed copying. They needed very few props, a piece of wood for a gun, a stick for a sword and their vivid imagination and memory of the story was all that was required. A suitable location for all situations was easily found in or around the town. There was the Common with its high gorse bushes and open spaces for the cowboys and indians. Surrounding woods and Love Lane were ideal places to re-enact the jungle adventures while many an historical duel was fought on the Castle Hills. Gangsters like Al Capone and Scarface lived over and over again in the streets and alleyways as boys raced noisily in pursuit of each other carrying their make believe pistols or Tommy guns. Some of the older children took this a stage further and formed their own gangs, usually from those living in the same vicinity and would then despatch a note [carried by a boy too young or frightened to refuse] to the leader of another gang declaring war or making some pretentious demand. This was generally all harmless fun but there was the odd occasion when one or two individuals got over excited and a little too rough resulting in minor injuries being inflicted by sticks or stones.

In the summer older children who were able to swim spent much of their time down by the river laying on the bank when they were not swimming in the water or playing games. Mothers took the younger members of the family to the shallow stretches like the Train Bridge on the Common where the water flowed crystal clear over pebbles. It was only about a foot deep so the children were able to paddle wearing an old pair of shoes to protect their feet from any sharp stones or broken glass from bottles and jars which might have been carelessly thrown into the river. Small fishing nets attached to a long bamboo stick could be bought at the Bazaar in Earsham Street for a few pence and with one of these and a jam jar, carried by a handle made by tying a piece of string around the top, many pleasant afternoons were spent catching the gudgeon which abounded and could be clearly seen swimming against the tide.

All generations of children get into mischief at some time and those of this decade were no different. When they were left to amuse themselves they sometimes found there was little to do and it was at such times they looked for excitement. When the fruit was on the trees it always looked tempting to youngsters who had insatiable appetites so it was not surprising certain orchards and gardens were targeted. They might start by grabbing a few windfalls before running off and then, as they found they were undetected, with increased courage they would select and climb the best trees to stuff their shirts as full as they could before making a getaway. Most of the people who owned the fruit probably didn't look on it too seriously so long as the trees were not damaged although they soon gave chase if they saw the youngsters and if they did manage to catch anyone they would dole out punishment on the spot in the form of a clip round the ear or kick up the backside.

Many houses had their front door directly on the pavement and children would playfully knock loudly on the door then run away as quickly and quietly as possible. Particular people were often the target for this kind of behaviour. Children are not only cruel to each other, at times, many pass through a phase when they seem to derive pleasure in tormenting those least able to stand up for themselves. There were one or two older women in the town who lived alone and kept themselves to themselves, they only went out if it was really necessary and when they did with their bent forms dressed in long dark clothes, a grubby shawl thrown round their shoulders and a large wicker basket swinging in their hand, they shuffled quickly on their way. They had only cats for company and youngsters overheard their parents relating jokes and tales about them which they quickly passed on to their friends. There were also a few men in the town who fell in much the same category and all, regardless of sex, were subjected to the same treatment from a number of children who would be rude and shout insults at them. Their doors were constantly knocked on and all sorts of rubbish put through their letter boxes. It was considered unlucky to see them in the street unless you rubbed a button on your coat or clothing with a forefinger. Rag and bone men, tramps and other underprivileged people were treated by some youngsters in the same way but fortunately such children were in a minority.

Sweet shops like the Bazaar where all the goods were laid out to view were a great temptation to any child and although punishment was quickly administered when someone was caught stealing it would be difficult to determine how many bars of toffee and chocolate were slipped into a pocket undetected. Even jars of sweets in some shops proved to be insecure and had a wire netting frame erected between them and the customers. The crimes committed by children were mostly petty and dealt with on the spot or in the evening when the father arrived home from work and heard the details. The most serious offences were likely to be stealing [borrowing] a bicycle, breaking windows or something along those lines.

There were the scouts, guides, a club called the 'imps' and other worthy organisations but they were only able to help a very few of the young people in the town. Older boys formed their own football teams and played home games on the common supplying their own kit with one side wearing white shirts and the other any colour and if there was any doubt one side played without any shirts at all. Away games were local enough for the team to be able to reach the ground on their bicycles.

Life was much different for the children from better off families. Although they were brought up under much stricter control and only associated with other youngsters approved by their parents they had many more ways of passing their leisure time. From an early age they enjoyed having new toys, there were dolls for the girls with all the clothes and accessories that went with them, the pram and cot could be almost as big as those used for a baby. All had teddy bears and cuddly toys when they were very young and as they got older most of their other toys were made of wood. There were things like rocking horses, horses on wheels hobby horses, trains and animals to pull along on a piece of string, many different carts and building bricks, dolls houses, jigsaw puzzles and lots more. It was not long before boys were looking to their birthdays and Christmas for such things as their first Hornby train set, box of tin soldiers, meccano set or farmyard set, all of which could be added to at a future date. The trains were clockwork and the accessories available which could be added to the set were almost unlimited, with every kind of passenger carriage, goods truck, stations, bridges, signals and signal boxes, points, crossings, sidings etc. This toy, more than any other, seemed to interest the fathers although many a happy hour was spent constructing something with the meccano sets which could also be added to with parts of all shapes and sizes and a battery driven dynamo so models with moving parts, like windmills, actually worked. Almost every regiment was depicted in the boxes of tin soldiers presented in authentic postures with every detail carefully painted in. Similar sets of cowboys, indians and troopers, many on horseback, were popular with a lot of youngsters. The farmyard sets too were made of metal and unfortunately very easily broken. There were barns, cart sheds and all types of buildings as well as fences, trees, hedges, ponds for the ducks and geese and every sort of cart and wagon that was found in the country. The animals came in all postures with some horses harnessed to fit into the carts. Care had to be taken not to drop any of these or apply too much pressure when it was necessary to straighten a leg so an animal would stand up as the brittle metal soon snapped.

Children from these families were able to keep their stamp

collections going after filling their first small book. Their parents were also able to afford any sports gear they needed, in many cases they required it for school anyway. Both St Mary's Church and the Congregational Chapel had tennis clubs and provided courts where the older children played in the evenings or during the school holidays and girls attending St Mary's School had a court in the school grounds and played hockey on the Common.

During the Summer months the family had outings when the children were often allowed to take a friend with them. It might be to the seaside or just for a picnic, or sometimes the friends were invited round for tea when, if the weather was suitable, the table was laid outside so tea could be taken in the garden. Whatever it was, manners and behaviour at the highest level were essential if the children expected to be allowed to invite anyone again at a future date. On birthdays and at Christmas they had parties when many friends and acquaintances were invited, the choice being that of the parents rather than the child concerned and would often be someone from a family they wished to impress. This might be held at home if the house was large enough but often a hall was hired for the occasion. Jellies, blancmange, biscuits, chocolate rolls and many other mouth watering goodies followed a variety of sandwiches after which they indulged in all sorts of competitive games as the hosts did their best to make it the most memorable and best party of the year. Acts like Punch and Judy or a magician were often hired and usually met with the children's approval.

All families took regular walks together and as the children became old enough a bicycle would be high on their list of 'wants' for a Christmas or birthday present and it was not unusual on a Summers evening to see a family of three or four setting out together for a ride in the country.

One week plus the bank holidays was the only time most people had off from work and the better off families made the most of this by going away for a week. They did not go far and living in Bungay they had easy access to the coast with a wide choice of resorts and accommodation which would most likely be in a boarding house. The more adventurous were being attracted to the holiday camps which were springing up all over the place but these estabilishments were not decorous enough for the upper middle class and in any event would be certain to have a bad influence on the children. However their popularity quickly grew in the later years of the decade as more people found themselves, for the very first time, in a position where some such luxuries were now within their grasp.

SCHOOL HOLIDAYS. RELAXING AT THE STAITHE

# CHAPTER 8.

## THE SHOPS AND WORKERS.

After they had finished their schooling a number of boys and girls found work in the shops in the town. When a vacancy occurred any boy who had previously been employed as errand boy for an hour each day after school and Saturday mornings had the advantage of being known to the manager and other employees but he would still have to show he had the educational standard necessary to be able to deal with prices and weights and measures as well as having the personality to cope with all kinds of customers. Many of the shop managers started this way and they were considered to have done very well for themselves. Most girls stopped working soon after they were married but there was always those who remained single and they would be likely to stay with their employer for many years. Some of them were promoted to take charge of departments or to other positions with responsibility like the cashier in one of the larger shops. As cashier they would sit in a small cash desk, usually near the entrance, receive payments, give receipts and do the accounts. All kinds of shops had assistants serving behind counters and in the smaller family businesses the assistant would take the money in exchange for the goods and give any change which might be due from a drawer under the counter or a box where the money was kept on the shelf behind him. In the larger shops, the assistant gave the customer a slip on which was entered the price of the items purchased and this then had to be presented with payment to the cashier who in turn issued a receipt.

There were several small grocers serving each area of the town with larger stores situated in the main streets, The Co-operative Society, Cox's and Haward and Dawson in Earsham Street, the International Stores in St Mary's Street and Brewster and Balls in the Market Place. Ring, a family grocer was situated in St Mary's Street. All the assistants wore white aprons or coats and although scoops were used, a great deal of the food was handled. In the larger stores groceries were to be found on one side of the shop with the bacon counter and butter etc. on the other. Preserved food could be bought in packets or tins but almost everything else was weighed and wrapped by the assistant. The scales they used varied, some were just balance scales where the appropriate weight was put on one side and the goods measured to match it on the other. These were very accurate so long as they were kept clean and nothing from the previous customer's order was left on them. Others were more sophisticated with a large hand visible to both sides of the counter which indicated the weight and if you were aware of the price per pound it was possible to follow a line of figures down the hand to see the the cost of the goods being weighed. Unfortunately the assistants using these all of the time became very proficient and were usually so quick the average person didn't have time to see what the price was.

Blue bags were supplied for different quantities of sugar which was weighed on the scales, tipped into the bag and then, after bumping it a couple of times on the counter to settle it down, the open top was folded in a very precise manner to ensure none spilled out. Tea, like many other things was tipped from the scales onto a piece of paper laid flat on the counter, the two outside edges were brought together and folded down, then one open end was raised and tucked in before the whole thing was turned over, bumped on the sealed end on the counter to settle it down and the other end secured in the same way. All of the shops packaged certain goods this way and paper bags were used sparingly on such things as biscuits and sweets. In some instances, for sweets and smaller quantities of things like currents and raisins etc. the assistant would wrap the flat sheet of paper around his hand to form a cone shaped bag which was secured by twisting the bottom where it came to a point. When filled, the top was folded down in the same way as the sugar bags. Bacon and ham was sliced as required and wrapped in greaseproof paper while butter and lard was taken from a large block with a pair of wooden paddles and patted into a small square shape before being placed onto a piece of greaseproof paper and weighed. It was amazing how near to the exact weight they were able to guess this before having to add to it or take a piece off.

Biscuits were displayed in front of the counter in large square tins with glass lids so the contents were visible to make it easier for the customers to choose which they wanted. The tin on the end was usually reserved for broken biscuits which were sold off at a reduced price and proved to be very popular with children who found them to be good value when they had a penny or two to spend. Needless to say when there were children in the shop the lids on all tins were kept tightly shut as their position in full view of everyone presented a big temptation to any youngster.

Women carried their shopping in wicker baskets or bags. Those using bicycles had a basket attached to the handlebars or behind the saddle and similar ones were available to fit on prams and pushchairs to make it easier for mothers with young children to carry their packages without having them pulled open or thrown onto the pavement. All the grocers delivered orders free of charge to customers in the town and many living on the outskirts who only shopped once a week were pleased to take advantage of this. Some households had a food safe outside to keep food such as meat and fish as well as their milk cool when the weather was warm. This was no more than a box with perforated sides to allow the air to pass through and was usually hung on the wall of the house facing north to ensure it was always in the shade and placed high enough to be safe from cats and vermin. In really hot weather households who had no such facility stood their milk in a bowl of cold water to help keep it fresh.

One way grocers helped their customers and themselves was by running a Christmas club. People paid whatever they could afford each week and had the amount recorded on a card so they were able to see at a glance how much they had at any time and plan how to spend it on their Christmas fare. Some shops gave a small interest on the total as an encouragement. This was just a way to help families to save and in many cases, if they did not put money away like this, they had nothing with which to pay for the extras everyone looked forward to during the festive season. Throughout the year, whenever a few pence could be spared the housewives bought a tin of salmon or fruit or something which was only ever seen on the table at Christmas to store away. The poorer families who shopped at the Co-operative Society and were members collected stamps with each purchase to stick into books provided or gave their number to the cashier when they paid their bill and the money they accumulated this way was either exchanged for goods when a book was full or put into a bank book where it earned a dividend. The latter was another way of putting a little away each week for a special occasion. There was a nominal charge made to members for the number they were given on joining and this was sometimes more than people were able to find.

Large stores like the Co-operative Society and Cox's sold furniture, linen and clothes as well as groceries and some of the smaller shops in the town also sold more than one type of product. Wightman, situated in the Market Place had departments for ladies clothes, linen and furniture as well as giving a service making funeral arrangements while Wightman in St Mary's Street was a gents outfitter with separate departments for shoes and the uniforms they supplied for the pupils attending Bungay Grammar School. Whyte's sweet shop in Earsham Street and Inwards the baker in St Marys Street both had adjoining tea shops. Smith the tobacconist was also a seed merchant and Short the newsagent in the Market Place had a print shop on the premises where all the local jobbing work was done.

There were shops in the town to supply the every need of the householders as well as hardware and ironmongers where tradesmen could get every kind of tool and accessary they required to carry out their business. Nuts, bolts, screws, knobs and handles etc. were all kept in wooden drawers under and behind the counter or in boxes stored on shelves reaching up to the ceiling, so steps were needed to get to them. It was a mystery how the assistants knew where to find anything for although some drawers and boxes were marked, many had nothing at all to indicate what was inside. Paraffin, white spirit and things like cresote were kept at the rear of the shop and some of the lesser called for items in the cellar which had an entrance through a trap door situated in the shop floor just in front of the counter. Ring the grocer had a similar cellar under the shop floor where bags of flour and sugar etc. were stored and before opening the trap door a rather flimsy rail resembling a wooden clothes horse was placed around it to keep people away from the hole in the floor when it was open.

No matter if you bought a pound of nails, clothes from an outfitter or almost any type of goods, it was more than likely they would be wrapped in brown paper torn from a large roll which was contained in a holder usually fixed on the end of the counter. Some of the bigger shops had this supplied with their name printed at intervals across the roll so it appeared on each parcel they wrapped. All packages were secured with string which was pulled from a spool usually suspended overhead with the end hanging down onto the counter ready for use. Bags, which were always made of paper, were expensive and used mostly for small items and foodstuffs. Shops and business people sending parcels through the post or by train ensured they would not be tampered with by covering the knot in the string with sealing wax into which they stamped their name or sign while it was hot and soft. Long thin wax tapers were used to melt the sealing wax which was always supplied in red coloured sticks.

Most people relied on the roundsmen calling at their homes for paraffin and hardware [there were three of them working in and around the town], for it was messy as well as being dirty and smelly to carry with you especially if you had other shopping to do. If it was necessary to go to the shop for it you always had to take your own can as they kept it stored in large tanks with taps from which the cans were filled.

Shops selling different kinds of goods all had their own familiar smell. Tobacconist, newsagent, baker, hardware, chemist and butcher to name a few. As you entered a furniture store you were met by the smell of rolls of colourfully patterned linoleum standing on end in rows which mingled with that given off by the freshly stained and polished woods as you moved further in. The new lino had to be handled with great care when it was fitted and laid because much of it cracked and tore easily if was accidently folded over. The smell persisted for some days after it had been laid and when it had been down a short time it settled and tended to stretch so if it had been laid to fit tightly to the walls it would have to be trimmed all round again and the process of lifting it could easily result in it being damaged. Furniture was delivered to customers on a two wheeled handcart bearing the name of the proprietor, with each piece carefully wrapped in a blanket or sheet, kept specially for the purpose, so they were not knocked or scratched in transit.

More people were employed at the Chaucer Press than anywhere else in the town and twice a day, ten minutes before they were due to start work in the morning and after they had been home for dinner, a steam hooter was sounded to remind them of the time. This was also appreciated by many of the town's other residents who relied on it for a time check. As well as books they produced many important journals and magazines on a regular basis. This gave a constant flow of work particularly for the 'jobbing ship' in the composing room for although they had both monotype and linotype setting, much of this work had to be hand set with illustrations, colophons and rules inserted. These were printed from type imposed and locked in chases on flat bed machines with the paper fed in by hand.

Books requiring long print runs or constant reprints had moulds taken off the type from which plates were made. These could then be nickel plated when runs in excess of 50,000 copies [depending on which machine, the paper quality, number of make-readies etc.], would be printed before they showed sufficient wear to warrant the making of a further set. To make the moulds, a paste was mixed using flour and water and pasted alternately onto layers of tissue paper and blotting paper. This was kept moist overnight then laid onto the pages of type securely locked in their chase and beaten into the characters with special hard flat brushes, after which they were covered with a blanket and subjected to heat and pressure under a moulding press where they became hard and dry. These moulds were then placed in a casting box and had melted stereo metal poured onto them to form the plate. When cold the back was planed and the edges bevelled and trimmed. With paper between each one to avoid damage these were much easier to handle and store than pages of type which had to be tied with string and placed on a piece of stout paper or card when removed from the chase and were so heavy only one page could be handled at a time whereas as many as thirty two plates were stacked in a pile and carried with ease.

Books with half tone illustrations and some which were often reprinted were produced from electro plates. These were made by covering the mould with a silver spray before hanging it in a copper bath so that a thin copper deposit completely covered it. This was peeled off and backed with metal then planed to the correct thickness before being slabbed on the back with special tools to make it level and flat. This was a very skilled, expensive and long process but copper faced plates were probably the best surface to print from and the hardest wearing.

There were printing machines to suit all kinds of work from a single page to large perfectors capable of printing 64 pages at a time with 32 on each side of the sheet. All sheets had to be folded and collated and this was done in the bindery where girls did a great deal of it by hand, especially for the journals and magazines. Others sewed the sections together ready to be put into their blocked cases and wrappered in a printed jacket or to have a limp cover put on. Every book was handled many times during its production and each one examined carefully before being packed in brown paper parcels to await transport to the railway goods station.

The Chaucer Press had it's own social club for employees where they could meet for a drink or to play snooker, darts or table tennis. Dances, socials and whist drives were held in the main hall which had a stage where pantomimes, supported by R. Clay, as well as plays and events organised by others in the town were put on and performed before the general public. One very important facility offered to members was the use of the baths for very few had anything other than a tin bath at home. After work on Fridays regulars arrived with their towels tucked under their arm to await their turn for a hot soak.

The jobbing printer in the town was very different to the Chaucer Press. Everything was done by hand and all the various stages of production were carried out by the same person and printed on the only hand operated press they had. When a job had been completed and delivered the pages were broken up and the type sorted in it's case ready to be used again. They held the colophon blocks which belonged to customers and headed all of their work. These were mounted on wood to make them the same height as the type so they were easily inserted into any new setting. The Olland Press was the other printer in the town, situated on the corner between Scales Street and Outney Road. They produced a news sheet which carried advertisements and was given away free. It was circulated to many houses and for those who did not receive one some of the shops had them on the counter for people to help themselves.

Butchers tended to specialise in one kind of meat and did their own slaughtering. Cold storage space was very limited so to ensure their meat was always fresh they would kill twice a week on Mondays and Thursdays. At the start of the decade they were not subjected to the use of the humane killer so cattle and sheep were pole axed and pigs had their throats slit. This was not as cruel as people imagine as the butchers who carried out this task were experts at their job and it was done as quickly and painlessly as possible. There were shops like Martin's in St Mary's Street and Bingham's in Earsham Street who sold beef and mutton as well as all kinds of birds and game with the latter on show hanging outside the shop window. Different cuts of meat hung by large hooks from overhead rails so customers could choose which they wanted. The one they selected was taken down and placed on a wooden block for the butcher to cut a slice or joint from it as required. The block was usually positioned in the centre of the shop and was solidly made with thick strong legs to withstand heavy blows as the butcher chopped and sawed through large joints and bones. No part of the animals was wasted so offal, lard, suet etc. were always on display in the window.

Chase in St Mary's Street and Bedingfield in Lower Olland Street sold only pork and specialised in their own sausages which they claimed contained a secret ingredient. They were certainly popular but this was more likely to be because of the price than anything else. Pork cheeses were another favourite and these were displayed in their enamel dishes on a marble shelf inside the window. There were various sizes with prices ranging from two pence to about a shilling each. When the butcher had processed everything from the pig only the scraps remained and these were cooked in a large pot over an open fire at the back of the shop and people called to buy them while they were still hot for a penny or two to take home for their tea wrapped in a piece of greaseproof and white paper.

In Cross Street the London Central Meat Company had a shop which only sold New Zealand lamb. All of the butchers were easily recognisable by their overall and striped apron and some had a steel slung around their waist ready to put a razor sharp edge to their knife. Every shop had clean sawdust spread on the floor each morning and swept up in the evening before closing when all the knives and saws etc. had been washed and the block and shelves scrubbed thoroughly. The floor was then given the same attention. Like the grocers and other trades the butchers all delivered meat to their customers carrying their orders in a large basket on the front of their trade bicycle.

The New Theatre and later the Mayfair cinema employed several people as they were open six nights a week with two performances on Monday and Saturday evenings and a matinee Saturday afternoon for the children. The programme changed on Mondays and Thursdays and there was always something special for the youngsters to see. Seats were bookable but this only applied to the better seats including the four rows in the balcony where the back row, like the back row downstairs had double seats which were obviously favoured by courting couples. The cinema was very popular even though the films shown were quite old before they arrived at Bungay. On occasions when a famous star was appearing a full house was expected and it was not unusual for late comers to be turned away.

The manager and his wife did much of the work themselves and were often seen issuing tickets or showing people to their seats. Bills were posted around the town to advertise the films for the week and in addition large coloured posters were designed and painted by the manager. These were put up each time the film changed on hoardings situated between the electric light shop and the telephone exchange in St Mary's Street and on a hoarding opposite the high path in Staithe Road. These were so big they were produced in as many as four seperate pieces which had to be fitted together to make up the complete poster. The man putting them up arrived at the site with them rolled up under his arm and carrying a bucket of paste with a long handled brush sticking out of it. One piece of the poster was held against the board while the back was pasted, then it was turned, put into position and pasted generously on the front. Other pieces were put up in the same way until the poster was complete. The whole operation only took a few minutes and was made to look a very much easier task than it really was.

Almost every street in the town had its own cobbler working from his home so he had no official hours and was always pleased to accept work even when others had finished for the day. He sat on a low stool and removed old soles and heels and nailed on new ones while the shoe or boot he was working on was pulled tightly onto his last which he had positioned between his knees. Soles were usually leather but some people preferred rubber heels, held on with about four nails, for these could be bought and replaced by any handyman with access to a last. If a working man's boots or shoes had leather heels the wear could be prolonged by putting two or three blackies at the back. These were small metal plates made with points on the back which were hammered into the leather. Boots worn by men doing heavy work often had hob nails hammered in all over the soles as well to make them last longer.

Not everyone could afford to have their shoes repaired as it was quite expensive so it was not surprising they were sometimes worn until there was a hole right through the sole. A piece of stout cardboard would then be placed inside the shoe to get a bit more wear out of them. Pairs of rubber soles to nail or stick onto existing leather soles appeared for sale in the shops and were available to fit all sizes of shoes but these really needed to be nailed or stuck to the original sole when the shoes were new otherwise they soon came away at the toe and were easily pulled off. They certainly saved the wear on the original sole but added to the cost of new footwear.

Anyone with a light or indoor job who was able to afford it, could have their shoes repaired with the leather sole sewn on by hand using waxed thread. A hole was made and one end passed through it, when the next hole was made a loop of the thread from one side was pulled through for the other end of the thread to be passed through it, both ends were then pulled tight to form a similar stitch to that of a sewing machine. This called for more skill and took longer than nailing or sticking soles on and obviously cost more so although most cobblers were able to do this there was little demand for sewn soles. They were however often asked to repair handbags, money pouches carried by roundsmen etc. and other leather goods.

All of the bakers shops made regular deliveries to their customers in their bread carts which were pulled by hand. The roundsman with his leather money pouch slung over one shoulder, transferred sufficient loaves from his cart to a large wicker basket which he carried on one arm to take the bread from door to door. The cart, covered in with two doors giving access at the front above the shafts, was left at the side of the road, the roundsman first making sure the doors were shut so the bread was kept dry and clean. Some people lived near enough to go to the shop where a selection of freshly baked cakes and sweets were a constant temptation. Bakers all made their own bread and cakes daily and for a few pence were always willing to pop a cake in the oven for a customer when they had finished doing their own. This was a big help to those families who only had an oil oven or had to light a fire especially to heat an oven built into the kitchen wall.

One of the shops with it's own very distinct smell was the tobacconist where much of the odour came from the shag which was kept in large jars and weighed out in ounces or even half ounces as required. After weighing, it was tipped from the scales onto a flat sheet of paper to be wrapped in the same way as the grocer wrapped his tea. A cabinet displaying pipes of all shapes and sizes was on the counter together with some fancy petrol lighters. Lighters were used by some but because they constantly needed filling and the flints had to be adjusted and renewed most smokers used matches. It was often said the taste of the cigarette was spoiled if lit by a lighter and cigar smokers would not consider anything other than matches. Many men and an increasing number of women smoked anything from a clay pipe, which was still enjoyed by many of the older men, to scented Turkish cigarettes which were tipped and rolled in all different coloured papers. These were favoured by some middle class ladies who wished to make an impression when they attended their social events. Small machines could be bought to 'roll your own' but most men found it more economic to roll them with their fingers as they were able to adjust the size of the cigarette to the time they had to smoke it. There was a sincere belief among all classes that smoking was good for you, especially for steadying the nerves if you were upset or under pressure and the only ill effects they were likely to have was to stunt your growth if you started too young and make you short winded if you were a sportsman. When the shops were shut cigarettes were readily available from public houses or from one of the slot machines which could be found outside several of the shops in the town, inside the clubs or on the railway station.

Many skills that had been practiced for generations were on the wane through the 1930's. The wheelwright had been on call for every kind of vehicle but with the decline of the horse he, like the saddler and blacksmith, found there was less and less demand for his services. It was good to watch the blacksmith at work, to sniff the smell of the forge and hear the regular banging of his hammer on the anvil as he shaped a shoe and then the sizzle of the steam which rose when it was plunged, still red hot, into cold water. Youngsters always seemed fascinated when, wearing an old piece of sacking around his waist, he lifted and held the horses foot between his own legs and placed the hot finished shoe onto the hoof sending up a small cloud of smoke as it was melted on to give a perfect fit before being nailed. Some wheelwrights were able to turn their hand to carpentry and joinery as their work disappeared but the saddlers had to depend heavily on the farmers who were going through hard times themselves and had harness repaired or replaced only when they really had to.

One business which was destined to survive no matter in which direction things progressed was the undertaker but even they changed the horse drawn hearse for a motorised one. People in Bungay had a wide choice of services offered by Biles in Scales Street, Wightman in the Market Place, Botright [also a carpenter] in Upper Olland Street and the Co-op in Earsham Street. Relationships within families were very important and strict guidelines which involved all the family and close friends had to be followed when one of them died. There were women in the town who could be called on to wash, dress and lay out the body soon after death and all other arrangements were made by the undertaker. The deceased was laid out in a spare room so those who wished to see them and pay their respects could do so and they remained there, in their coffin when it was made, until the day of the funeral. During this time the whole family was in mourning and to indicate this the blinds were left down over the windows all day. The women wore dark clothes and covered their heads when they went out and no member of the family was expected to indulge in any sort of social activity which could be interpreted as pleasure. Black arm bands were quickly bought or made and worn by all the family while those men that wore them donned a black tie. On the day, the hearse was followed from the house by all the family and close relatives who were preceded by the bearers appointed by the undertaker who walked with them suitably dressed in a long black coat and top hat with a black ribbon draped around it. As the procession moved down the road, pedestrians and vehicles of all kinds stopped, the men removed their hats and everyone faced the road in silence until the cortege had passed.

While the funeral was taking place one person, usually a neighbour, always remained at the house and made sure everything was ready when the family and friends returned for refreshments. This might consist of a cup of tea and a cake or, in more wealthy households, a glass of port and a mince pie. Such occasions were often the only time families all got together. Most people paid insurance to cover such eventualities and they needed to for the cost was high for even the most simple ceremony. If the family could not pay or there was no next of kin the account had to be settled by the council, in which case costs were kept to a minimum. The undertaker had several people to pay including a driver, the bearers, the clergy for organist, bellringers etc. and the gravedigger as well as the cost of the coffin and hearse. The stonemason was another man involved when the family was one of the better off and able to afford a head stone.

A few men and women were employed in the various offices in the town where records and accounts were kept in hand written ledgers often in duplicate or even triplicate. All were done in ink using a pen holder with a nib which would have to be replaced almost daily if in constant use. A pencil was used for invoices, delivery notes etc. as these were duplicated by using carbon paper and pressure had to be applied to get a good impression. Wax crayons were ideal for marking the outside of parcels for identification and in cases like registration through the post a blue line was drawn around both ways to form a cross on the top and bottom. It was not easily rubbed off and was unaffected if it got wet.

These people were often much better paid than manual workers and the more responsibility they accepted the more privileges they were given. Their day started later and finished earlier so they worked less hours and, depending on their length of service and seniority, they were given extra holidays and some qualified for a pension when they retired. More important, it was the prestige that went with these jobs that attracted many who applied for them and any openings were keenly contested. Factories and businesses tended to keep paperwork to a minimum and employed as few white collar workers as they could as they were considered non productive. The Post Office, banks, insurance offices and the railway offered good opportunities to those with the necessary educational standard but in almost every case, for people living in Bungay, it meant working away from home.

Second-hand shops always seemed to be busy with nobody really sure just how much business they actually did. They were always willing to buy [at a very low price] as well as sell almost any kind of article. There were one or two shops operating in the town as well as the rag and bone men who called round at regular intervals and would take away almost anything you might want to get rid of but only at his price. Then there were people like Mr Vincent who lived and operated with his brother from their house in Turnstile Lane. They were always dressed in shabby black suits with long jackets which had slits up the back and large patch pockets. Their waistcoats, shiny from wear and dirt, had a watch chain attached to a buttonhole with the watch tucked securely into one of the pockets. Their faces were almost hidden by long scraggy unkempt beards beneath black broad brimmed hats and they could often be seen pushing an old pram, which had long since lost it's hood and was now used to transport anything they might buy or be trying to sell. Needless to say most people declined to open the door if they were aware it was them who were knocking on it for their reputation did little to encourage anyone to do business with them.

Many different kinds of goods were taken round the streets and up to people's doors for sale. Besides the regular roundsmen there was the gypsy with his pegs, the dark skinned man wearing a turban with a large suitcase filled with colourful scarves and clothes, the man with a bag full of household cleaners and dusters, the fishmonger with his handcart loaded with all sorts of fish including shrimps, cockles, mussels, winkles etc. and the corona man who called every week delivering soft drinks in many flavours supplied in returnable bottles which had a stopper secured with a wire clip to make it easy to reseal after it had been opened and keep the gas in so the contents didn't go flat. The ice cream man on his three wheeled bicycle was never far away and was always a welcome sight on a hot sunny day.

Many other kinds of shops and businesses thrived in the town and all played an important part in the everyday life of the people. The atmosphere in the public houses and at the market or the fish shops with their smell and the sound of fish and chips frying as people crowded in when the cinema and pubs closed for a pennyworth of chips and a piece of cod or plaice, as well as the feelings experienced everywhere else at this time, reflected the mood of the people and highlighted their determination to enjoy and make the most of what they had while they struggled for something better.

LOWER OLLAND STREET

BRIDGE STREET

# CHAPTER 9.

## LAW AND ORDER.

All generations have had to tackle the problem of apprehending and punishing those who break the law and the method of doing so has to be changed constantly and updated as society progresses and criminals become more and more sophisticated. At this time towns like Bungay and the surrounding villages had the local policeman to depend on to maintain law and order. He walked the beat around the town and used a bicycle when it was necessary to travel longer distances as did the village bobby who had several miles of country roads and lanes to cover every day.

These policemen, who were dedicated to their duties, found that what they were called on to do gave them more a way of life than a job. They were generally family men and were provided with a police house which often served as a station and meant they were on call twenty-four hours a day. What time they had to themselves seemed to be spent in the garden where they were frequently seen in their shirt sleeves, braces pulled off their shoulders and hanging down their sides, depending on their belt to hold up their trousers as they dug or hoed to provide vegetables for the family and in some cases to nurture produce to a high enough standard to enter the local shows.

Their uniform was thick and warm with the silver buttoned tunic done up to the neck. The chain from the whistle in the top pocket visibly attached to a buttonhole with a notebook and pencil bulging from the pocket on the other side. A truncheon was carried in a back trouser pocket and the uniform was completed with a stout pair of leather boots and the traditional helmet secured with a strap under the chin. This must have been warm and comfortable in winter but very hot and uncomfortable in the summer months. They had overcoats when it was really cold and waterproof capes to put on in wet weather which they often rolled up and tied on the handlebars of their bicycle. The policeman in small towns and villages were a special breed of men who were not there just to maintain law and order but were well thought of and highly respected and always available to give friendly help and advice to anyone who asked for it.

As a result of the town's high degree of independence the council and leading citizens had quite a big say in the methods adopted to prevent crime and apprehend offenders. People who broke the law and were caught expected to be fairly treated and suitably punished with a sentence to fit the offence. Bungay had it's own Courthouse situated in Castle Orchard [behind Ling the chemist in St Mary's Street] where suspected criminals appeared before the magistrate who, in minor cases was able to pass sentence and in more serious cases commit the offender to a higher court. The maximum prison sentence that could be awarded by such a court was six months and in the event of the person convicted feeling dissatisfied with the hearing or the sentence they were able to have their case heard in a higher court. Much of the magistrates time was taken up dealing with petty crimes and disagreements and had it not been for the understanding and efficiency of the local police they would undoubtedly have had many more cases to pass judgement on.

The police in Bungay, with a resident sergeant in charge, operated from the police station in Priory Lane where they had two cells always ready for immediate use. With the restricted transport and communication of the day most of the crimes committed were done by local people which put the responsibility for finding the culprit entirely on the local police. Strangers, who were always looked on with suspicion anyway, would have difficulty getting away without being spotted after committing a felony within such a small community where faces were all familiar. Everyone knew the sergeant and he made it his business to know the right individuals, those he could call on for help and information as well as those most likely to commit an offence.

There were the well known and harmless rogues who never missed an opportunity to make a shilling or two and the habitual thieves and poachers who found a ready market for the game they caught and who freely boasted of their achievements but rarely seemed to get caught. The local police also got to know those most likely to have too much to drink and create a disturbance when the pubs closed and they were not usually far away when they were required to break up a fight or see a drunk safely on his way home. A friendly warning to all first time offenders, like publicans serving drinks after hours, was usually enough to prevent any escalation of law breaking.

The police at this time also had a very good understanding of youngsters who all went through the stage when, if the opportunity presented itself, they would help themselves to sweets or anything else that caught their fancy. Most boys scrumped apples or fruit at some time in their lives and although youngsters got up to all kinds of mischief they did not often do any malicious damage, at least nothing worse than seeing who could throw stones onto the roof or break the most windows in a derelict building. When the first Belisha beacons were used on pedestrian crossings on the roads in the larger towns and cities, it was reported that the flashing yellow lights had soon become a target for young hooligans who took delight in smashing them with stones. Although there were no beacons on the roads in Bungay, a few of the more rowdy children did throw stones at the new electric street lights in an attempt to smash the bulbs and so put them out. Such actions were generally the result of high spirits and youngsters leading each other on in search of excitement and perhaps it was not quite as bad as using birds or rabbits as a target for their missiles or daring one another to commit some mischief to prove their courage. One thing was certain they were always fully aware of the punishment they would suffer if they were caught. Knowing this, in some cases, only added to the thrill of what they were doing.

The police, when called in, invariably hauled the guilty children before their parents who would administer the appropriate punishment either physically with a belt, slipper or just a hand, or by restricting their freedom and finding them extra tasks to do in their leisure time. For a more serious crime the headmaster of the child's school might be involved and it would have to be something very grave and perhaps an aggravated offence before a youngster was charged and taken to court to be dealt with by a magistrate or judge. The intention, shared by all concerned, was to find a just punishment which was sufficient to deter the culprit from repeating the offence. There was no thought of analysing their motives or giving corrective training to show how they should fit into society. In all probability most of the children liked it that way. If you did wrong and were caught you took your punishment and then the whole matter was forgotten.

For the ultimate crime of taking a life there was the death penalty and other serious offences could be dealt with by corporal punishment or hard labour or both. For less serious crimes there was prison or fines. There were those who were not really criminals but got caught up in circumstances beyond their control which brought them before the magistrate. People who were homeless, perhaps turned out of their home by bailiffs because they were unable to pay their debts or a young man or woman turned out for any one of a dozen reasons, with no fixed abode found it was against the law to sleep in the streets and if they were caught they were arrested and consequently charged. Those members of the community unable to fend for themselves who came before the magistrate might very well be sent to the

Workhouse at Shipmeadow, which some seemed to dread while others did their best to get in, or perhaps an alternative similar charitable establishment.

There was always those ready to take advantage of the law and in bad weather it was not unknown for a tramp or vagrant to purposely get themselves arrested and put in the police cells for the night where they knew they would be given a meal and a warm dry bed even if it was only a hard wooden bench in a locked cell. This was an example of the kind of circumstance when the policeman's discretion and knowledge of the local people was called on to ensure no one was able to make a habit of doing such things as this.

Poaching was something many tried their hand at with some having more success than others. Gamekeepers were unable to patrol their entire estate all the time and it was after dark and preferably on a clear moonlight night when the poachers were most active. Men from poorer families might do it simply to provide a meal for their family while the professional did it for a living. Snares were popular and readily available from Gibson and Balls in the Market Place who employed women and girls to make them in a room above their shop. Some steel traps were used but they were considered to be very cruel. Many poachers depended on finding a bird perched in a tree or bush asleep so they could creep up, grab it and wring it's neck before it had a chance to cry out. Needless to say this required a good deal of luck as well as skill and more birds struggled free and flew noisily away than were found on the dinner table next day. Those that set snares had to return the following night to see if they had caught anything and there was always the chance of the gamekeeper finding them the next day when he did his rounds, in which case he might well be waiting when the poacher came back to check. Rabbits were often caught using a ferret. A net was put over the bolt hole and the ferret, with his mouth tied so he couldn't bite or kill it, was put down the hole on a long lead. If the rabbit took fright and bolted it was caught in the net, if it didn't it would hunch up in the burrow with it's back to the ferret who could only scratch at it with it's claws. Their position in the burrow was determined by the length of lead let out and the noise they made and a hole was dug down to the rabbit with a spade so it could be taken out of the burrow.

As well as birds and rabbits fish were poached. There was no salmon or trout in the river but it was well stocked with eels which were very much in demand. A legal eel trap alongside the sluice at the Falcon Meadow was dropped and the gate holding up the water opened so as the water rushed through the eels were caught in a steel grating. This was always done on Sunday mornings during the season and the catch was then transferred into a box with a wire netting top, tied to a stake on the bank and submerged in the water where the eels were kept alive and fresh until they were collected and taken to market. Anyone holding a fishing licence could catch them with a rod and line or a bab while some preferred to tie a fork onto a broom handle and go round the shallow dykes stabbing into the bottom where the eels had buried themselves in the mud, until they struck one. On a good night they could fill a bucket this way and arriving home they would cover them with salt then leave them for several hours to remove the muddy taste before they were skinned ready to cook. River bailiffs regularly patrolled the banks to check and catch the people fishing without a licence. These were not very expensive but like the licences required to keep a dog or own a wireless there were always those who thought they could get away with not buying one or just couldn't afford it. Failure to produce fishing or other licences resulted in a small fine.

It was against the law to net fish in the river but this was done by some individuals who found a market for the eels they caught. To keep them fresh until they had sufficient to make a worthwhile sale they kept them in a small pond which had been dug out on the Grammar School Meadow. Situated on the river side of Staithe Road behind the houses, the meadow stretched to the rear of Trinity Church. It had been neglected for several years and was overgrown with all kinds of trees and plants. That is, all except an area big enough for two tennis courts which had been cleared at the rear of Trinity Church and used and maintained by St Mary's Tennis Club. The entrance to the courts was through large green gates on the high path and a narrow track had to be negotiated through the undergrowth to reach them. Just through the green gates, in the wall on the left, was a large iron gate leading to the kitchen garden which was still dug and planted and maintained in good order. This gate, secured with lock and chain, had not been open for quite some time which was just as well, for if it had, the fresh garden produce would have been as big a temptation to the poachers as the eels. It is unlikely they used the green gates where they might be seen entering for access to their pond. They were less likely to be detected if they crossed the adjoining meadow behind Inward's garage further down Staithe Road and crawled through a hole in the hedge.

Gypsies and other travellers were moved on as quickly as possible after their arrival in the town because, although it may have been untrue, it was readily accepted they were responsible for anything that went missing during their stay and there were always those waiting to take advantage of such a fact. Some moved around the countryside with planned regular stops to coincide with events they could benefit from such as Bungay May Fair where they had a chance to buy and sell while others hawked their wares from door to door. One of the best known was Gypsy Gray who visited the town regularly and as well as telling fortunes if her hand was passed with silver, was reputed to offer for sale goods she had bought from Woolworths for less than half the asking price. People bought them whether they wanted them or not just as they did the bunches of heather and wooden clothes pegs the gypsies became well known for simply because they were afraid not to. Although most people dismissed as nonsense the threats and curses which were put on them if they refused to buy anything, many admitted feeling disturbed and upset after suffering a verbal assault from one of them and preferred to avoid it.

Of all the varied crimes the police had to deal with one of the most common and difficult was theft. Within certain societies there are different categorys of stealing while the law recognises only one. Poorer people in a close knit community would find it unacceptable for a man to take anything from his neighbour under any circumstances without permission but if he stole from a large organisation such as the railway they were likely to rally round to prevent him being caught. This attitude was not confined to Bungay and applied to all walks of life throughout the country but was obviously more prevalent among the poor and underprivileged.

A typical example of this was on the trains when it was found to be impossible to open the carriage window because the long leather strap used for that purpose had been cut off. As most local trains did not have corridors in their carriages and some doors only opened by the handle on the outside this caused distress to the passengers wanting to alight who could only hope to attract the attention of the porter or guard as they walked down the platform before the train moved out of the station. The leather straps were ideal as a strop on which to sharpen the cut throat razors still used by many men who shaved themselves. Anyone finding it necessary to visit the toilet on a corridor train or the station might find the towel and toilet roll missing. The fact both would have been clearly marked L.N.E.R. was no deterrent for even if people had no water closet the toilet roll was something of a luxury compared to the squares of newspaper which were cut up, secured by passing a piece of string through a hole pierced in one corner and hung on a nail, which is what many people had to make do with.

Lots of pilfering went undetected and even when it was discovered a great deal of it was never reported. Sometimes the identity of the culprit was obvious and they confessed as soon as they were challenged, like an employee stealing from the till. Such cases might be dealt with on the spot by instant dismissal or, with all the circumstances considered, it might be decided that with reimbursement another chance should be given. Times were hard and some people were hungry so it was not surprising when vegetables were reported missing from allotments or the odd chicken from someone's back yard and although the offender was often known, it was difficult to produce proof so he might well get away with it.

Sweet shops, particularly the Bazaar in Earsham Street, who had their goods laid out on a very wide counter were very vulnerable and a great temptation to children of all ages. In some cases they dared each other to go in and see who could steal the most. The boys, wearing a belt, found it easy to slip things into their shirt where they could not be seen, particularly if they were wearing a jacket. For girls it was not quite so easy unless they were wearing a coat as their frocks and jumpers and skirts were usually without pockets. Some did have a pocket for a handkerchief on the leg of their knickers but this was too small to be of use so they would most likely conceal any sweets etc. they stole up their knicker leg until they got out of the shop.

The small sweet shop and general store in Lower Olland Street was originally owned by 'Bumper' Reeve then Read [an Irishman who also did an oil round with a pony and cart] and later Emma Rumsby. This was soon a target for youngsters who could easily reach the jars of sweets to lift the lids and help themselves having first sent her to the rear of the shop for something they had no intention of buying. When they had taken all they wanted they ran quickly from the shop. The same children would return again a few days later knowing Emma would readily forgive them and never dream of reporting them to get them into trouble, although later a wire netting frame was put around the sweet jars to prevent children taking the sweets. Unfortunately there were also adults who took advantage of such a kindly nature and it was not long before people she allowed to run weekly accounts, some of them just for cigarettes, failed to pay for several weeks and then stopped calling and seemed to disappear. In addition Emma was over generous on her scales when she served children. The result was that she struggled to make a living from what could have been a prosperous business.

On occasions like race days the police were reinforced with both regulars and specials and extra vigilance was necessary to combat the more professional criminals like pickpockets who came into the town to mingle with the crowds. Their main duty was to direct and control the crowds but there were constant diversions when their services were called on to attend to other more urgent and serious matters.

Bicycles were a constant target for thieves and owners had to make sure they were stored securely when they were not being used. It was not only the habitual criminal who was likely to take them if they were left unattended. Anyone missing the last bus home at night faced with a four or five mile walk would be very tempted. More so if there were two of them and they were slightly the worse for drink. It was a common sight to see someone on a bike carrying a passenger on the crossbar although this was later made illegal. After dark bicycles had to have a light on the front, usually in the centre of the handlebars but some like the tradesmen's cycles with a carrier on the front had a bracket fitted on the hub of the front wheel to hold it. It was also compulsory to have a red reflector on the rear mudguard. Both battery and carbide lamps could easily be removed as could the pump which most cycles carried clipped to the frame and these were frequently stolen no matter how careful the owner might be.

People leaving their bicycles to shop, go to the cinema or just call on someone, no matter if it was day or night, had to take with them all accessories that could be removed if they didn't want to lose them. Even the bell which was screwed to the handlebar and the tool bag strapped to the back of the saddle were frequently taken. It was always very difficult to apprehend the people who did this unless they planned to do it just for profit and returned to the same place repeatedly. Although it seems to do so would be foolish, any habitual thief operating in a small town had a very limited number of places where there was likely to be opportunities so from time to time they were caught and became known to the police and consequently considered for any similar crime committed in the future. The ones who got away with it most of the time were the opportunists who were passing, saw something they wanted and took advantage of the chance on the spur of the moment to take it, probably never having done anything like it before and perhaps never ever repeating such an action.

During hard times such as these there were lots of honest people driven to commit all sorts of misdemeanours out of keeping with their character in their efforts to support their families. One serious consequence of this was the effect it had on the family. Children's understanding of right and wrong was mainly influenced within the family circle and it was important parents guided them by example as well as instruction.

Bungay had it's share of minor crimes and the odd more serious one. Generally it was kept under control and people were reasonably safe walking the streets and in their own homes where, even after dark some never bothered to lock their doors or bar their windows.

CHAPTER 10.


THE RIVER AND THE COMMON.


The days when the wherries transported goods to the town and unloaded at the Staithe were long gone as were the locks between Bungay and Beccles so that stretch of the river was no longer navigable. Above the sluice and the mill it flowed north of the town all around the Common and under the bridge approaching the town from Earsham to pass on the south side, thus forming a peninsular. In the past this might have been an asset in ensuring the town's independence and making it easier to defend but now it was an obstacle to it's progress. As new houses were planned to replace the old small congested dwellings in the streets and lanes there was only one side of the town on which to build and even there some of the land was marsh and not suitable, so a thriving market town was obliged to confine it's growth within existing boundaries and suffer the consequences.

In one way or another the river and the Common played a part in the lives of everyone in the town. The Common was really divided into three, the lows where the cattle and horses grazed, the Big Common with it's race course and golf greens, and the Little Common where the public enjoyed the fairs and circuses when they visited the town. The two commons were divided by the railway track and access to the Big Common was over the wide railway bridge with it's brick walled sides which had spiked rails on the top to stop the children climbing up on them and falling over. The brickwork was always black with soot deposited by the smoke as the engines passed underneath. On either side at the foot of the wall was a wooden board, presumably for people to stand on and watch the trains as they puffed in and out of the station and which children found gave a hollow sound to their footsteps as they ran over them to go through the side gate onto the Big Common. To ensure no animals could stray off and no unlawful vehicles could get on the large gate was kept locked and the side gate was held shut by a very strong spring requiring an adults weight to push it open, at which point most youngsters jumped on it for a ride as it closed with a bang.

It was generally believed the Common belonged to the residents of Bungay and could only be taken from them by an act of Parliament but each time the question was raised there was little evidence to support this and there was a charge for grazing on the lows or riding a horse on the Big Common. Besides which, the golf club and others using any part of the Common paid dues to the owners, who were never identified, through their solicitor. When an attempt was made to clarify the situation the people enquiring were advised there was nothing could be done as the deeds had been burnt some time in the past. However the public insisted on their right of way and although someone went as far as to put a chain and lock on the gate it was only a very short time before it was cut off and access restored to everyone. The issue of who received the revenue for the various activities was often raised and discussed but never resolved. At some time before the thirties gravel had been extracted leaving pits, now overgrown by grass and gorse, behind the two grandstands. These stood on high ground from where there was a full view of the whole race course with it's numerous jumps including the water jump which was situated right in front of them. One of these stands was more recently built than the other and some years later it was dismantled and re-erected on the Maltings Meadow for the use of Bungay Football Club.

The golf house was popular and much used by those who could afford to and the natural course and greens, laid out so as to avoid the race track, was enjoyed by many more. Some only had a couple of clubs and others even shared in order to learn the game. A professional was employed at the club to give lessons and train those who wanted help and had the necessary funds to meet the charges. In places across the Common the gorse was very thick and high and elsewhere the grass beside the course was long which resulted in many lost balls. The Common was a favourite place for many to exercise their dogs and it seemed inevitable that one of these on his early morning run would develop a knack of finding lost golf balls and fetching them back to it's master who had no trouble finding someone to take them off him in return for a small reward.

Wild life and the flora were in abundance for all to see and enjoy. In Spring, a step or two off one of the recognised paths into the longer grass was likely to put a skylark to flight from it's nest in the grass. Once hovering overhead it would give it's familiar call. Rabbits were in evidence everywhere and the odd stoat and grass snake as well as lizards and other smaller creatures could often be seen. Other than the rabbits, which some men set out to catch, the wild life was undisturbed and suffered only their natural enemies for only the grass on the courses was cut and kept under control. Elsewhere the Common was left in it's natural state and this large flat gorse covered area, with hardly a single tree, sloping down to the lows and backed by tree lined hills on the other side of the river presented a beautiful view at all times of the year with the multicoloured flowers and grasses merging into the various shades of green and brown.

At the top of the first slope, about a hundred yards from the gate, the council had a chrome drinking fountain erected with a concrete base laid in a triangular shape and surrounded by an iron rail. This was particularly welcomed by everyone in the Summer for when the sun shone on a still day the common was a very hot and dry place. Seats were placed nearby so older people could rest comfortably or mothers with young babies could attend to them without having to sit on the ground to do so. Others liked to just sit there and watch the young families at play with bats and balls and when the wind was right, enjoy seeing the energetic actions of fathers teaching their children the rudiments of getting a kite up in the air and flying it. Beyond the drinking fountain, surrounded by a post and wire fence, was the pump house where water was drawn to supply the town from the almost inexhaustible quantity to be found beneath the Common. Villages nearby took advantage of this and purchased water. Ditchingham was supplied through a large pipe across the river, just high enough to allow boats to pass underneath.

Sitting on the seats at the top of the first slope looking down to the golf house was a good position from which to watch the hockey matches played by the pupils of St Mary's School. Their goal posts and corner flags were stored in a shed at the rear of the golf house and had to be got out and erected by the players before the game could start and no one was allowed to leave when the game was over until they had been safely locked away again. The golf house standing alone and being hidden on one side by the high fence which separated it from the railway station was often a target for robbers and vandals.

Further along the high wooden fence was replaced by a wire and post one where it was easy for parents to sit with their children and watch the trains as they ran in and out of the station. As long as the wind was blowing off the Common there was no danger of getting covered in smoke and smuts. If they were fortunate a goods train might arrive with wagons destined for Bungay and then they could watch the engine shunt the wagons into position to be unloaded in the goods yard.

It was alongside this part of the fence the cricket club had their small pavilion where they met to practice in the evenings or dressed in their whites to play a match on Saturday afternoons.

The surface of the ground was not really good enough for hockey or football never mind cricket but they made the most of it with the square concreted and a coconut mat laid between the wickets.

At the Broad Street entrance to the Big Common the gates were much the same as those at the Outney Road entrance. Situated over the railway crossing the large one was kept locked and the small one held shut by a strong spring. Here it was even more important they were never left open as the cows from the smallholding and milking parlours were turned out here. Early in the morning and by three in the afternoon they would all congregate around the gate waiting for someone to fetch them and take them home for milking. If they were let out accidently or pushed their way out with those belonging to someone else they would simply make their way down the road and across the Market Place or wherever they had to go to reach their shed. Once there they made straight for their own stall and manger and the food which always awaited them. Not many of the public used this approach to the Common for obvious reasons, it was always very muddy under foot and they were not keen to push their way past the cows who, although harmless, are always very inquisitive and likely to cluster round a pram or pushchair and have been known to even lick the occupant with a rough wet tongue.

The entrance to the Little Common from Broad Street was on the left before the railway crossing and was not much used except by the locals walking their dogs round the block or taking a short cut to the station. Most people used the Outney Road entrance as they did for the Big Common and golf house. This area of land was the ideal site for a visiting circus or fair. It was just the right size and out of the town but not too far away and enclosed with a hedge on one side and the railway track on the other. Using the Big Common for such events after dark would have presented risks to children and adults alike, for once away from the glare of the lights it was difficult not to lose ones sense of direction and on a moonless night it would be easy to walk into a ditch or gorse bush and once lost a child in panic could very easily run into the river. Even courting couples did not venture too far away from the gate unless it was a clear night. In later years the printing works slowly swallowed up the Little Common right up to the railway track without the public seeming to be aware they were doing it.

Although there were times when it was treacherous all kinds of people enjoyed the river in many different ways. Some liked it for the fishing, others for swimming and boating while many found it relaxing to just sit beside it and watch the gentle flow glistening in the sunlight as younger people romped and skylarked on the banks. There were several favourite places where they congregated when the weather was warm. The Falcon Meadow where the sluice and eel trap held up the water for the mill stream was always popular, particularly at the weekends when people of all ages brought their chairs and blankets to sit on as they watched others swimming and diving into the hole off the walls of the eel trap or over the bushes on the bank. The hole was dug out by the force of the water over the sluice in the winter when the river was in flood and was said to be between fifteen and eighteen feet deep.There was always a challenge among the teenagers to see who could dive down and bring something up off the bottom for it was very dark down there so everything had to be found by feeling for it. There were some surprising objects picked up and brought to the surface from time to time. On one occasion it was a tin of worms discarded by a fisherman or dropped in accidently and on another it was a small sack tied with half a brick attached containing three drowned kittens which was certainly not dropped in accidently for this was how some people disposed of them when they were unwanted and the hole was as good a place as any to do it. A little further down river the debris dug out of the hole piled up so when the water was low it formed an island. On the down stream side of this the schools and parents taught children to swim. Nobody was considered a swimmer until they had swum across the hole from the island to the eel trap which was only about twenty yards but a test of any youngster's nerve as well as ability.

Swans dominated their own waters and were to be seen at all

times of the year occupying almost every part of the river around the Common and beyond. They were a protected species and their numbers seemed to increase every year but they were no trouble and everyone enjoyed seeing them gliding gracefully on the water with the cob and pen ever watchful over their sygnets. Many stories were told about the strength and power of their wings and how they could break a man's leg with one stroke but generally they were harmless and would come to the bank and sometimes out of the water to take bread from your hand. Passing them in a boat with oars splashing might produce angry hissing as they lifted themselves out of the water and one well known cob called 'Billy' had a way of swimming down the river away from you then, when he was far enough, he turned and with wings flapping noisily and feet trailing in the water he came straight at you. Fortunately he always seemed to stop just short of the boat and then slowly lower his feathers and return to his family. This was a frightening experience for many especially if they had heard the tales of how he had once capsized a boat when he flew into it and on another occasion killed a dog who was barking at him from the bank. Nobody knew if these stories were really true but they were often related and made some people very wary how they approached any swans.

Sandy, another popular spot for swimmers, could be reached from two directions. The quickest way was to cycle over Ditchingham Dam and turn off down the lane which led to Baldry's and Bath Hills. The other was to cross the common to where the cut to Baldry's harbour, workshops and house created an island which was covered by tall trees. On the edge of these were five or six wooden bathing huts, erected by Mr Baldry, for hire. Most of the younger generation however preferred to undress on the bank on the Common side even though this meant scrambling up a muddy bank to get out of the water as the only steps were on the island side. A new concrete and iron footbridge was built across the river joining the Common and the island by the then Town Reeve. The water was not too deep here and most of the older children were able to stand in most places on the sandy bottom. One drawback was, being open to the Common, if there was any wind blowing you got the full force of it and it sometimes felt warmer in the water than it did when you came out of it. The youngsters solution to this was to indulge in energetic games or romp about on the bank. One game, sometimes known as 'high cockalorum', was quite popular and played by two teams of any number. The members of one team bent over to 'make a back', one behind the other tucking their heads in and holding on tightly to the person in front. The other team ran and vaulted onto them one at a time until they were all on with nobody touching the ground. The first team then had to hold them while they all chanted 'high cockalorum chick chick chick' three times. If they collapsed before this was completed the second team had another turn.

Another pastime was to run a few hundred yards across the Common to the 'Hot Country' which was a large round area of sandy soil devoid of any kind of grass or plants and which it was claimed was always warm and you only had to dig down a few inches to reach water. The latter might well be true but the only time any one was likely to run over to feel the earth was in the summer when the sun was shining.

Further up the river, where it widened on an S bend, was Finch's Well where Finch was supposed to have drowned many years before. This was another place favoured by some strong swimmers and reputed to be a bottomless hole which joined the waterways under the Common. It was certainly deep and diving down the water became very cold and dark quite suddenly, so much so that no one was foolish enough to try to reach the bottom as they did at the Falcon. A rope tied to the branch of a tree on the Ditchingham side gave a great deal of fun to those brave enough to swing out over the hole and drop off into the water. There were lots of stories about this particular spot and the people who had supposedly drowned here and although they were repeated with disbelief like fairy stories many people passing on their way up or down river sat very still in their boats and looked anxiously at the water to try to determine exactly where the hole was. Almost everywhere along the river, weed and in some places the bottom was easily discernable as were the fish as they swam by in the crystal clear water but where it got deeper as the bends approaching Finch's were reached, the water became very dark and nothing could be seen through it.

On the other side of the Common a few people swum in Toby's hole which also had a nice sandy bottom to one side of it where the water was shallow enough to stand up. Like Finch's Well, this had a story told of it. Toby, driving his pony and cart homeward, after a long session in one of the local pubs, drove straight into the river at this spot and was never seen again.

Further upstream was the railway bridge where the water was only knee deep in places and ideal for young children to splash about in or just paddle and catch tiddlers. Children went in the water dressed in a pair of pants or knickers and the very young without anything on at all. For them it didn't matter, but there were laws governing dress for adults on the beach at the seaside and swimming which were strictly adhered to everywhere and some swimming pools had their own standards which were even more conservative. To start with both men and women wore complete costumes, no two piece for the women and no trunks for the men were allowed. Most were made of cotton and many to the same design. They were held up by straps which buttoned over the shoulder and black or navy blue from the waist down with a brighter coloured top which might have stripes or hoops. No one seemed to consider or take any notice of how revealing they were when they were wet and the swimmer left the water. It was not long before the men all changed to trunks and the women appeared in costumes of many different colours and designs many of which were probably copied from those worn by the stars in the Hollywood movies. Two pieces consisting of shorts and a top which tied behind the neck and round the waist leaving the back and the midriff bare appeared as a dress for leisure and sunbathing. It was not long before the two piece swimsuit and the bikini were being worn and tolerated almost everywhere.

Many keen anglers relaxed on the river bank watching their float bobbing up and down as a gentle breeze blowing against the slow moving tide rippled the surface of the water. They had their favourite places, on a bend, in the mill stream, where a dyke ran into the river or under the trees where they would be most likely to get a bite. An occasional boat might upset them by tangling their line around an oar if they were slow reeling in or if they didn't see them coming, other than that and the odd inquisitive cow sniffing at their bag there was little to disturb their tranquillity. There were roach, perch and dace as well as eels to be fished for and for the more energetic there were always plenty of pike to challenge and tease onto the hook as the spinner was repeatedly cast and reeled in. In the summer when the water level was low and the sluice on the Falcon Meadow was dry, many elvers were to be seen wriggling up the concrete slope to drop into the water at the top as they made their way upstream. As one would expect, children thought it great fun to catch them and have races on top of the wall but no matter which way they placed them it was soon evident they would only move in the direction pointing upstream.

On fine warm evenings during a hot spell in the weather, one or two men who lived close by, generally those employed doing dirty jobs, arrived at the river bank with a towel and trunks in one hand and a bar of soap [probably lifebuoy] in the other. Quickly shedding their clothes and donning their trunks they chose a shallow part of the river where they were able to sit down and soap themselves all over. If they were at the Falcon Meadow the bottom of the eel trap was ideal, they could sit in a couple of inches of water with their legs submerged hanging over the edge. Once they were completely covered in soap rinsing was easy, they just dived in for a swim round. This was obviously more pleasant and far more efficient than washing in a bowl in the kitchen or backyard as they normally did. Although it was sometimes hardly discernable there was always a tide flowing downstream so little concern was shown for the the suds which soon floated away. There was a theory often quoted by those who frequently used the river that so long as the tide was flowing the water was safe to swim in without any fear of contacting anything which might be detrimental to one's health. With the amount of garbage disposed of in the river and the rubbish often seen floating by it is understandable these people needed some sort of a boost to their confidence from time to time.

One of the most relaxing ways to pass the time on a fine and pleasant day was to sit back comfortably in a boat while someone rowed it slowly up the river. Only boats propelled by oars or paddles were to be found on this section of the Waveney. Power boats were not allowed as the marshy banks would be too easily eroded and in any case, at most times there were many places where the water was shallow and any propeller would certainly get fouled by the thick weeds. There was no restriction on sailing except that the river was too narrow for it in most places. There were adequate facilities nearby at Beccles for those who wanted to take up this sport. The nearest thing you would see resembling it around Bungay was perhaps a twin canoe with a small sail rigged, steered and assisted with paddles or youngsters in a small rowing boat where the river widened at the bottom of the Common on a stretch called Blackwater, with an old blanket for a sail and an oar lashed to a thwart to serve as a mast. Their progress was very slow but no doubt they had lots of fun.

Rowing boats were hired out by Clarke's from a yard at the bottom of Bridge Street where there were five or six available. It was more popular to set out from was Baldry's where there were more than a dozen varying in size to take no more than three people in the smallest one and up to eight in the largest when two sets of oars were provided. The cost was about a shilling an hour which, paid on return to the harbour, was charged to the nearest quarter of an hour. The boats were all built by Mr Baldry in his workshop where he used steam to bend the planks round the ribs to make a traditional clinker built hull, a long and very skillful operation. Later, when he was older, he produced one or two using sheets of zinc for the hulls as these were much quicker to make and easier to patch up if they got damaged, which they did from time to time. Anyone could hire a boat if they were over sixteen [this was one of Mr Baldry's own rules, I believe]. For many leaving the harbour it was a first attempt at rowing or steering and with little or no idea of how to keep the boat trim they were a great source of amusement to onlookers especially when they steered into the bank or 'caught a crab' and finished up sitting in the bottom of the boat while their oars floated away down river. Needless to say all losses and damages had to be paid for. Cushions were provided to sit on as the thwarts became very hard and uncomfortable after sitting on them for an hour or so.

Once out of the harbour there was a choice of going down river as far as the Falcon Meadow where the sluice prevented any further progress or upstream where, if you had the time, it was possible to travel right around the Common to the train bridge and beyond. Not many went so far, it was more usual to take a snack or picnic and find a shady spot under the trees where the boat could be secured and everyone relax while they eat their food. Target, which was a part of Bath Hills situated up river beyond Finch's Well, had always been a favourite place to stop and while the older members of the party rested on the bank the others would attempt to climb the hill. This feat was only accomplished by clutching and holding on to the roots and branches of the trees and shrubs as you tried to gain a foothold and pull yourself up far enough to reach and grasp the next root or branch on the path you had chosen to climb. A slip or a broken branch could result in a slide all the way down to the bottom, for the hill, with a surface of clay, was very steep and slippery with deep channels running from top to bottom cut out by heavy rain as it flowed down to the river. A spell of wet weather made it almost impossible to hold your feet at all and quite a dangerous feat for even the fittest to attempt.

Neither the river nor the Common were as attractive in winter as they were in summer for even on a dry bright day a cold east wind was likely to be blowing up the Waveney Valley and billowing across the open common. It didn't seem to deter the golfers or those who wrapped up and exercised their dogs every day no matter what the conditions were like. For most people however, when the days were short, the weather bad and much of the ground underfoot wet and soggy, the Common was not the place to be.

An exception to this was after a heavy snowfall when all kinds of people appeared from nowhere with sledges and those that didn't have one made do with anything from a wooden box with a couple of runners nailed hurriedly on the bottom to an old tin bath pulled by a rope tied to the handle. The place they made for was the pits behind the grandstand where the slopes, largely covered in grass and gorse, had clear paths running down. These were kept open in the Summer by people walking down and youngsters on their bicycles seeing who could negotiate the steepest with the uneven ground at the bottom as a further hazard, after which they had to scramble up again with their bikes. If the snow on the slope wore thin more was thrown on as one after the other they pushed off from the top, hanging tightly onto their sledge as it sped down, sometimes into deeper snow where it had drifted against the foot of the hill and with most getting tipped off when they reached the humps and bumps. This was great fun for some adults as well as the children and none seem to notice the cold or the wet clothes from constant falling and rolling in the wet snow.

As the snow melted the water in the river rose and the flow increased, changing the friendly and tranquil stream into a dangerous, fast flowing and sometimes destructive torrent which affected people's lives in a very different way. Every year there was sufficient rain to cause at least part of the marshes to flood so animals had to be moved to high ground and the water frequently washed over the road on both the Earsham and Ditchingham Dams. At such times the town's home football fixtures had to be postponed until the water receded from the Recreation Ground. This was a problem they never had when their home pitch was on the Honeypot Meadow. Heavy snowfalls or a very wet spell coinciding with adverse winds and tides on the coast holding up the water made the flooding very serious and resulted in many roads being impassable. People living by the river and marshes were forced to move upstairs as the water rose and came into their houses, sometimes lapping at the door when sandbags helped to keep it out but more often seeping up through the floor when nothing could be done to stop it. At these times a good deal of everyday life came to a standstill as services were affected and villages cut off. On more than one occasion the water on both dams out of the town was several feet deep and forced people who lived on Ditchingham Dam to move upstairs in their homes.

One year the marshes were flooded at a time when the weather was extremely cold, in fact so cold that not only did the flooded meadows freeze over but so too did the river. It was soon discovered the ice was thick enough to walk on and people seemed to appear from nowhere with their ice skates, firstly on the meadow on Earsham Dam opposite the Recreation Ground, then as the ice got thicker they moved onto the river and some skated on the cut between the main river and the millstream at the Staithe. Several spectators assembled along the tow path to watch them as they sped to and fro with the odd one taking a tumble every now and then. This went on for quite a while until one unfortunate man, a reader at the printing works who lived near at hand in Staithe Road, went down with a heavy bump and went right through the ice, luckily there were lots of willing hands to pull him out and rush him home before he caught cold. The hole he made was right in the middle of the cut and there was just room to skate by at the side of it. When one brave man did so however the ice dipped and creaked enough to put him and everyone else off risking it again and so a few days offering an unusual opportunity to exercise their skills at a new sport came to an end.

The worst flood came toward the end of the decade when the water at the bottom of the sluice on the Falcon Meadow was level with that at the top and formed a kind of rapid as it rushed over in a torrent. The railway line, which was usually high enough to be unaffected, was partially washed away together with the road bridge alongside Ditchingham Station while a double decker bus, stuck on Earsham Dam when the water was rising, had to remain there while the water crept up over the seats on the lower deck until it was half submerged. Buses for Norwich left from Ditchingham Maltings and anyone who worked there or had business to attend to who wished to travel on them could cross the dam in a rowing boat at a cost of a shilling each way. As the flood began to recede one enterprising man did the trip for about the same price in a horse and cart which might have been a good idea for those anxious to get across but more than likely a terrifying ordeal for the horse, half submerged, as it struggled to keep it's feet. The only things seemingly unaffected by the floods were the swans who continued to glide gracefully over the surface no matter how deep or widespread they became.

After a day or two the the water level went down to reveal the damage done to property and crops in the fields which had been affected. Householders began to clean out any mud and dirt and assess what had to be done before starting the job of drying out their rooms. Most needed redecorating as the water mark on the walls was very difficult to get out. With such a flood parts of the road surface as well as the river banks and bridges were washed away and had to be repaired and it took some time before all the buildings and numerous gates and fences which had suffered or were missing were restored. It must have been particularly hard for people like Mr Baldry whose harbour and the lower half of his house and workshops were submerged and cut off for several days. The fish apparently stayed in the confines of the river during the flood and normally would not be likely to suffer too much but on this occasion, when the water receded, there were reports of many dead ones floating on the surface. It was said they were poisoned by the tar from the roads which had drained back into the river as the level went down.

Water attracts and fascinates young people at all times but never so much as when the tide is rushing by sweeping away everything that gets in it's path. Parents being fully aware of this, never ceased telling youngsters of the dangers associated with the river but such facts are always difficult for children to apprehend especially when they can so easily recall the fun they had swimming and splashing in the shallows with the stream flowing so slowly it was hardly discernable. It was inevitable, living with water almost all round the town, that accidents would happen from time to time. Unfortunately when they did no one was ever able to determine quite how or why such a thing occurred or how it might have been prevented bearing in mind there will always be children who are more inquisitive and daring than others. There were not many fatal accidents but those that did occur were far too much for a small town to bear. The whole population was devastated when a young life was lost, everyone being aware that under different circumstances it could have been their child.

THE FALCON EEL TRAP AND SLUICE

CHAPTER 11.


PASTIMES AND LEISURE.


People did not have much time to themselves during the week but most of those with a regular job had one half day off, shops closed at lunch time on Wednesdays while the majority of employers finished their week at midday on Saturday. This worked out quite well as it gave anyone who was unable to get to the town in the week a chance to do their own shopping and buy a few extras like fruit and sweets for the weekend, if they could afford them, for the shops remained open until eight thirty or nine on Saturdays.

The town was usually well crowded that evening with people bustling to and fro doing last minute shopping and the Salvation Army Band added to the atmosphere as they played and sang their familiar tunes under the Butter Cross while other members shook their collection boxes at passers by. Later in the evening they toured the pubs for donations and sold their copies of the 'War Cry'. Further down St Mary's Street, opposite the Catholic Church, there was often a street musician, shabbily dressed and unshaven, playing a flute or some other musical instrument with

135

his cap placed on the pavement in front of him to collect any odd coppers sympathetic people might throw in.

One of the busiest shops was the barbers as this was the time the villagers came in to the town to have their hair cut. There was only one style for men, 'short back and sides'. These words were usually mumbled by the hairdresser as he ran the hand clippers up the back of the neck almost to the top of the head. It often felt as though he was pulling the hair out instead of cutting it. The operation was not complete until a generous blob of Brylcream was massaged in and the hair parted and combed, then followed an inspection of the back reflected in the mirror from the hand glass held at an angle behind the head. The barber brushed away the bits of hair that had fallen onto the customer's shoulders and held his coat for him to put on while he opened his purse and took out enough money to settle up, generally including a small tip which they came to expect from regulars.

All the shops were busy even though a lot of people were content to just walk up and down the street talking and mingling with others. A lot of men who depended on their bicycle to get them to work and did all their own repairs and maintenance chose this time to visit the cycle shop to buy the things they needed and and seek advice. The tobacconists did a brisk trade as men called in to buy their cigarettes and tobacco for the week. Many of those who smoked a pipe bought their shag loose and put it into a special earthenware jar when they got home to ensure it stayed moist. Those shops which sold ice cream were also very busy when the weather was warm. Whyte in Earsham Street had Lyons Maid and had to unwrap the brick before putting it between two wafers or if you wanted a cornet the ice cream was round with a flat top and bottom and supplied with a thin piece of card wrapped around it which had to be removed before it was manoeuvred the right way up in the cornet. Walls bricks or ice lollies [these were only a penny] could be bought from the Tea Rooms in Cross Street or from one of the 'Stop me and buy one' bicycles which travelled all round the town. Paravani sold his home made ice cream from a horse and cart specially built for the purpose and Mrs Raven who kept the sweet shop in Lower Olland Street, which was the recognised tuck shop for the Grammar School boys, sold her own wafers and cornets with the home-made ice cream scooped out and spread onto the wafer or pushed into the cornet with a wooden spoon. These were just some of the ice creams available and each tasted very different but they were all delicious.

After about seven thirty people began to disperse, some went into the pubs where they might discuss the sports results and assess their local teams performance and prospects, others attended the second house at the cinema or went off to a dance, social or whist drive while for many it was time to make their way home calling for their fish and chips on the way. When the days were long and warm many of the younger citizens, some in pairs others in groups, strolled down onto Earsham Dam and sat on the pipe rail which ran through concrete posts on both sides of the road for the whole length of the dam. The favourite place was just at the bottom of the hill where they watched and greeted others as they passed on their way home or just taking a walk. The rail along this section became quite polished and shiny where people sat during the Summer.

Walking was a pastime enjoyed by almost everyone, particularly young couples who often had little else they could do. The common was the place they frequented most as it was large enough for them to be on their own and if they wanted more privacy there were lots of small clearings in the gorse bushes which were not visible from the recognised paths but easy to find if you looked for them. There were other popular places like Love Lane, a small path leading off St Margaret's Hill which was very secluded and hidden by trees. Any show of affection in public beyond holding hands or an arm was frowned on so it was not surprising youngsters looked for somewhere they could be alone. One place that did cater for them was the New Theatre which had a very small balcony at the rear and all the seats on the back row were double but when the Mayfair opened although they put some on the sides at the back they were only a few seats away from the gangway and not nearly as private or cosy. It was also unfortunate that these seats were the most expensive in the house and youngsters could not always afford them.

Saturday afternoon was the time for fetes, shows and jumble sales etc. organised to raise money for charities and so long as the weather was reasonably good they were well attended. Once it was decided to hold an event and the details had been worked out, the committee had the job of ensuring that anyone likely to support it was aware of the time and place it was to be held. This was mostly done by passing the word from mouth to mouth and posting bills which were each drawn by hand in coloured crayon or in indian ink using wooden pens of varying widths. These were pinned up on appropriate notice boards outside the church halls and around the town as well as in shop windows. They were more discreet when deciding where to hang them than the professionals when the circus or fair was coming to town for then every post and billboard seemed to carry one or even two or three of their posters together.

At many of the venues the British Legion had several stalls and amusements manned by their members or loaned out to other organisations.These included a small roundabout for young children operated by turning a handle and requiring more than one fit man to keep it going all the afternoon. Then there was hoop-la, quoits, knocking down piles of tins with a rolled up duster and darts as well as others and to add to the atmosphere and help to get people in a light hearted mood one of the men would turn the handle on a barrel organ which rendered a well known repertoire of popular old tunes.

Most local organisations had their own fund raising stalls with many of the members donating home made produce for sale and giving prizes for the raffles. While some of the public patronised the stalls others would be entertained by groups from various dancing classes and clubs keen to show off their prowess. The Honeypot Meadow was a popular place to hold these events while some preferred to use the lawn of one of the larger houses in the town with the kind permission of the owner who was likely to be a prominent member of the committee. Generally these occasions were a success and enjoyed by all but there were times when they had wet and cold days and were forced to hold the event inside and limit the activities to fit the accommodation which was likely to be in one of the church or chapel halls. These places were always in demand throughout the year for all kinds of functions from socials to jumble sales.

Saturday afternoon was the highlight of the week for all sports fans. There was always football or cricket on the recreation ground or common and sometimes other sporting events taking place on the Maltings Meadow. A few events might be organised for the evenings during the middle of Summer but all outside activities had to be completed in daylight so in the middle of the football season the final whistle had to be blown before three thirty or the game might be abandoned because of bad light. Billiards, snooker, table tennis and darts were all popular pastimes for members of the various clubs all the year round but those like the Chaucer Institute only catered for adults who were paid up members. The clubs for juniors, like the scouts and guides, had more specialised activities so youngsters who were keen on sport mostly organised their own by getting together with a ball on the Honeypot Meadow or the Common where they picked sides from as many as were there who wanted a game.

Tennis, like bowls and golf was for the better off. Not only did you have to pay a subscription to belong to a club, there was equipment and the correct attire to be bought so most of the working class was automatically excluded from such activities. Nevertheless they had their football to follow and many found a few pence to chance on the pools each week while the bookmakers welcomed all who enjoyed a flutter on the horses or dogs which they were able to do all the year round.

Whist drives were very popular with the women and some of the menfolk and was one method used by many organisations to raise money, some having them regularly every week. The prizes were very modest but no one seemed to mind and at one time they were even being held in the afternoons with all the prizes,amounting to no more than a tin of fruit or a bunch of flowers, being donated by enthusiasts. At Christmas and other special occasions drives were arranged with much better rewards offered for the winners and if you wished to attend these it was necessary to buy your ticket well in advance to be sure of getting one. All of these functions made extra money serving refreshments and selling tickets for a lucky draw.

Friday or Saturday nights were the favourite nights to hold dances and socials although all such events had to finish by midnight on Saturdays. Every week there would be at least one organised for the younger people to attend at the King's Head, the Three Tuns, or in one of the church halls when the music was often supplied by no more than three musicians playing the accordion or piano, the drums and a saxophone. The admission was between ninepence and one and sixpence depending on the size of the event and the band. People from the town were often attracted to the surrounding villages when they held dances and socials in their village halls.

Sunday was a day of rest and a very peaceful day with the quiet being broken only by the church bells which pealed for half an hour before the morning service began. A few men employed on essential services and those with animals to care for were obliged to work but for everyone else it was not only a day off but a time to relax. People felt very strongly about the sanctity of this, so much so that there were some women who would not knit or sew on this day and nobody would ever consider putting washing out on the line. There was a deterrent for some in that superstition decreed anybody performing such tasks on the sabbath would have the devil and bad luck with them all the week. Those that could afford to did have the traditional roast and Yorkshire pudding for dinner [the meat left over would be eaten cold on Monday which was a busy wash day], so those wives didn't have much rest, but a great number of the middle and the upper class families had a cold lunch when they returned home after church.

Those working class men who did not attend church might spend the morning on the garden or doing odd jobs around the house then go to the pub for a pint before dinner after which a doze in the chair or on the couch seemed a natural thing to do.There were those who took it a step further and went upstairs to lie on the bed for a couple of hours. When they reached the age of five many of the children were sent off to Sunday school in the afternoon and while their family were growing up this was sometimes the only occasion the parents found themselves alone in the daytime. Some of the youngsters continued to attend for years and progressed to bible classes which was their training for confirmation or went on to become teachers themselves while others left after a very short time. During the Summer months they all had a break and the afternoons were spent on the common or by the river with the parents relaxing on the bank while the children played and amused themselves stopping only for refreshment from the bottle of lemonade and perhaps a biscuit their mother had thought to bring with them.

Strict rules of behaviour for Sundays were laid down and followed by most of the middle class. All the family donned their best clothes and even if the adults did not attend church it is likely the children went to Sunday school and some of the boys who were members of one of the the choirs went to all the services. In any case they were not allowed out to play but the family might all go out walking together or take flowers to the cemetery to put on a relatives grave. Those with bicycles could take a ride around the countryside and view the farmlands and villages while the more ambitious youngsters had towns like Beccles, Harleston and Halesworth all near enough to be visited. At other times of the day and in the evening the family would sit together and read or perhaps, depending on the children's age, play a board game such as draughts or snakes and ladders and as they got older they might  be allowed to join in a game of cards.

Walking was something everyone did, partly because there was no other way to get where they wanted to go but also it was a pleasant way to relax and pass the time. There were recognised routes in all directions from the town and the one chosen would depend on how far you wished to go, the time of the year and who you were with. For instance, after the evening service a group of choir boys might agree to a stroll round the back of the hills or if they felt energetic, walk down Flixton Road along the Ups and Downs and when they got to the cemetery they could decide to carry on over Wooden Bridge, down Kent's Lane and home by Beccles Road or take a short cut up St John's Road. Senior members of the choir were more likely to want a longer walk and choose to go down Beccles Road round Wainford and home by Ditchingham. There was a short cut across the fields if anyone got too tired to go all the way.

There were popular walks to suit everyone from a stroll round the back of the Castle Hills to distances only enjoyed by those who were fit and used to walking. One route favoured by this group was to Homersfield via Earsham and back through Flixton. Those who really wanted a challenge set out across Ditchingham Dam, walked all round Bath Hills and returned through Earsham. In wet weather this could be a very hazardous and muddy journey. Although there were lots of routes to chose from many people preferred a leisurely stroll on the Common or the Castle Hills where they could take a rest and watch the children playing.

Newsagents and confectioners were the only shops allowed to open on Sundays and no organised sport of any kind was permitted but people were able to play golf and swim and many families enjoyed a picnic on the Common or by the river when the weather was good. When the weather was nice there was always a rush for Baldry's boats on Sunday afternoons. Some however would settle for the walk over to his place where they could buy a pot of tea and biscuits and rest awhile as they watched others leaving and returning to the harbour before deciding which route they would take for the walk back. Mr Baldry took bookings for those wanting to be sure a boat the right size was available when they arrived but it meant a walk or cycle ride over there earlier in the week to reserve it and you would have to take a chance on what the weather would be like. This was usually done if it was a special occasion and on the day the party would arrive with a basket or hamper filled with sandwiches, sausage rolls, cakes and other food for a picnic. They would moor up in the shade of the trees where it was easy to clamber onto the bank without getting muddy and lay out a blanket or cloth so, with the cushions from the boat to sit on, everyone was comfortable. Some even brought along a primus stove with a tin kettle and bottle of water so they were able to have a fresh cup of tea. This made everything perfect unless it was a wet and windy day when burning the methylated spirit to heat the jet before pumping it became very difficult. So did just keeping dry if you were caught unawares by a sudden shower in an open boat. The thwarts and cushions became soaked by the rain from which there was no escape or shelter. The only thing to do was laugh about it, which is exactly what most did as they rowed as quickly as possible back to the harbour from where they had to make their way home in their wet clothes. The weather however never seemed to deter anyone from going again on another day.

Swimming and frolicking in the water was a very popular pastime enjoyed by all classes. Some schools and parents chose Sandy as the place to teach youngsters to swim. It was considered safer and cleaner than other spots as it was shallow with a steady flow and there was less likelyhood of feet being cut on broken glass or other rubbish which was often thrown thoughtlessly into other parts of the river. Ladies too preferred it here as it had the facilities for changing and steps leading into the water.

When the weather was warm the Train Bridge was by far the most popular place for those with very young children. Women settled down with their books, knitting or sewing with their basket which contained food for a snack and a drink, perhaps lemonade for the youngsters and a flask of tea for themselves. Sometimes they packed enough food for a meal and made a day of it while the children swum, fished and played on the river bank.

Beccles had a swimming pool which was a part of the river boarded off and subject to much the same pollution and health hazards as were found in the open river but you did know how deep it was and there was someone responsible in attendance.

However there was an admission charge and many preferred to swim in the open river ignoring the fact the pool also gave them protection from passing boats some of which were power driven and a real danger especially to younger children. The citizens of Bungay had talked of having a proper pool built for as long as anyone could remember and in the mid thirties a firm proposal was put before the council to build a modern one on the site of the Honeypot Meadow. News of this was greeted with great interest and enthusiasm by the townspeople of all classes but unfortunately the council members were split on the idea and the proposal was finally defeated by just a single vote after which the public seemed to lose interest and became resigned to having to continue to make do with the river.

The New Theatre was built in the last century and started out as a theatre presenting shows by well known artists before it was converted into a corn exchange and later a cinema. When the new Mayfair opened to show films there was an attempt to use this building to bring back variety and music hall to the town. Sid Swain's party had been a big attraction in the old days and he was one of those who returned to see if he could regain his popularity with the audience. Karl Dane the strong man tried to attract people to his show by pulling a bus filled with school children with his teeth. He did this one lunch time opposite Barclay's Bank in Broad Street where the road was deemed to be even. Not only did he move it but managed to pull it, moving backwards as fast as he could, for several yards. Some plays were presented as well as variety shows and it was not surprising to find that one of the favourites was 'Maria Martin, Murder In The Red Barn'. Choral societies gave renderings for the public and other evenings were set aside for performances by lovers of light and other types of music. There were also occasions when, like the Chaucer Institute, this was the venue for an amateur boxing tournament.

The Mayfair was so well supported there were times they had to close the doors and turn people away. What loyalty there was for the New Theatre soon evaporated and it was forced to close.

However, it managed to struggle on a bit longer when all the seats were removed and it reopened as a roller skating rink. It was not really large enough and the wooden boards on the floor were very uneven but with everyone going the same way round they managed to maintain some sort of order. Most youngsters had to make do with a cheap pair of skates which were held on with two clips screwed in to grip the sole of their shoes and a strap fastened round their ankles. These were quite dangerous as the sole would often give way and the skate come off causing a fall and perhaps a twisted ankle. They had no ball bearings or springs and it was not long before they became twisted and bent so they continually pulled to the left or right. Nevertheless, despite the knocks and bruises, many who tried it enjoyed it enough to go back for more.

During the Summer most children had at least one outing to the seaside with an organisation they belonged to and many parents made an effort to take them, perhaps during their annual holiday, even if it was only for the day. Getting there was easy, it was the cost that deterred them. Trains ran regularly to Gt Yarmouth and Lowestoft, although you had to change at Beccles. If you had a pram or push chair the guard and porters would always lend a hand to transfer it from one van to the other. Cheap day returns were often put on at the weekends and almost every Sunday a coach, costing less than the train, would leave the Market Place for Gt Yarmouth in the morning and return in the evening. There was a problem if it turned out to be one of those days when the east wind blew relentlessly off the sea and it was cold and wet and you had a young family to amuse for hours. Walking up and down the front with little or nothing to spend, you tried to keep warm until the coach was due to leave. Such things were not usually considered and if they happened they were soon forgotten and only the good days remembered when the sun shone and parents sat in their deck chairs, which had to be kept in their rows, as the children made sand castles and paddled in the sea. Wooden boards were placed on the sand leading down to the chairs to make walking easier for everyone including the men who moved up and down the beach all day selling ice creams or fruit which they carried in a box or tray supported by a leather strap round their neck.

For those that could afford it there were donkeys to ride on the beach, a Punch and Judy to watch and all sorts of rides, side shows and attractions to amuse the children and their parents. If it was warm father might be enticed into the sea for a paddle for salt water was considered to be very good for the feet. With his shirt sleeves turned up over his elbows, his braces holding up his trousers which were rolled up to his knees and a handkerchief knotted in all four corners on his head to protect it from the sun, he would stand with his hands in his pockets and survey all around him as the waves broke gently on his feet. On the way back to catch the bus or train there would be a chance to sample a saucer of cockles or some other shellfish or even jellied eels from one of the stalls along the sea front while the children were likely to be content with a pennyworth of chips, some candy floss or a stick of rock.

TRAIN FROM BECCLES PULLS INTO BUNGAY STATION

# CHAPTER 12.

## EVENTS THROUGH THE YEAR.

Most people's daily routine was monotonous with little or nothing different happening as one day followed another. Nearly all their time and energy was taken up in the effort required to keep home and family together. It was not surprising that they looked forward to any coming event or celebration with excitement and enthusiasm. There was a strong religious influence on all festive occasions even among those who did not attend church and these were respected and observed by the majority of citizens from all classes.

February 14th. was of more interest to those in their teens and early twenties than any other age group as it was the day valentine cards were given anonymously with a message, usually [but not always] from a boy to the girl he most admired. All young ladies hoped to get an abundance of these but sadly many got none at all and even when they did they could only guess at the identity of the sender as this was never divulged. These cards, often home made, were not always posted and were more likely to be slipped into a school desk or left where it was sure to be found and passed on to the addressee. Younger boys had their own way of enjoying this day when, after dark, they set off with an empty parcel, wrapped and tied with string, and attached to a long piece of strong twine. A house was carefully chosen in a secluded area with the right layout approaching the front door. The parcel was then placed on the step and the twine carefully payed out as all but one of the boys concealed themselves in the darkness. When they were ready, they took up the slack on the twine until it was taut and the boy not yet hidden hammered on the door as hard as he could with the knocker or rang the bell and then hurried to join his mates to wait and see who answered. Opening the door and finding no one there the householder would look around for a moment before glancing down and seeing the parcel. As he stepped out to bend and pick it up the boys would give a sharp tug on the string to retrieve it and run for their lives. This seemed far more exciting to them than just knocking on the door and running away.

Lots of people of all ages made an attempt to give up something for Lent but very few of them had the resolve to carry it through until Easter. The most popular sacrifice was to stop smoking which had the added incentive of being a way of saving a few shillings a week. Like those that gave up sweets and other luxuries very few lasted the full course. Good Friday was a national holiday, although some trades like the builders worked on that day and had the following Tuesday off instead. This was a good enough reason to look forward to it but the highlight of the day was having hot cross buns for breakfast. These were ordered some time earlier from the bakers. By eight o'clock on that morning with the smell of baking wafting out of the shop doorway there would be a queue stretching down the road made up of both young and old from all over the town waiting to collect their order. The buns came out of the oven and were rushed home while still hot. The rest of the day was treated much as a Sunday but with church services in the morning only.

Any mention of Easter to a child brought only one thought to mind and that was chocolate eggs. None of them had any idea why they were given eggs to celebrate Easter Sunday and it was not likely any cared very much. They were never allowed to have them until Sunday morning and in some families they were then forbidden to eat them until they had finished their midday meal. As with other things some had more than were good for them while many children were pleased to have been given a few coppers to go up the town looking in the windows of all the shops who had them on display before deciding which one to have. There was no doubt in such cases that one small egg, which had none of the pretty silver paper wrapping, was a greater source of pleasure to that child than the half a dozen or so big fancily wrapped ones received by the children of better off families could ever be. Apart from the church's celebration Easter Sunday was treated much the same as any other Sunday except it was more enjoyable knowing the following day was a Bank holiday and you didn't have to work on that day either.

At this time of the year as days were becoming longer and warmer every household started to think about spring cleaning and deciding what had to be done. Living rooms and kitchens became very dirty after a season of burning fires and oil stoves. Both of these had a habit of smoking, especially if there was a slight draught or the wind was in the wrong direction and blew the smoke back down the chimney and into the room. This often happened, especially when the fire was first lit. More mess was made when the man called to sweep the chimney and pushed his brush right up and out of the pot to remove all the loose soot. Although he carefully covered the fireplace with a sack and laid a sheet on the floor to put the rods on as they were pulled down and unscrewed, a lot of soot always managed to find it's way onto every ledge and surface in the room. Cleaning the ashes from the grate every morning before laying the fire also sent dust flying everywhere. However, the dirtiest thing of all could be an oil stove or lamp if it was not properly maintained and the wick trimmed so it didn't smoke. On occasions, when unattended, a draught fanned the flame and the room quickly filled with thick black smoke which took a long time to clear. When it did it left a thick layer of greasy soot on everything including large cobwebs which seemed to be everywhere and until this time had not been visible.

The ceilings in these rooms were usually whitewashed and a roll of whiting from the hardware store mixed with water would be sufficient for quite a large room. First the ceiling had to be washed thoroughly when some of the last coat of whitewash would come off, then the whitewash put on evenly with brush strokes finishing toward the window. It had to be applied thick enough to ensure it dried up white but not too thick, for if it was it would start to peel off after a couple of months and then the whole ceiling had to be scraped right down to the plaster and done again. To do any of this without making a lot of mess was impossible and the walls would invariably have to be distempered or papered afterwards unless they were painted as they were in the kitchens of many houses, then they could easily be washed down with sugar soap which would remove any grease and dirt at the same time.

A job could be found for every member of the family at this time. Curtains were taken down, washed and put up again. Carpets [the stair carpet was often the only one] were taken up and put over the linen line for beating if they were small enough, otherwise younger members of the family took them to a nearby meadow or field where they were laid out on the grass and beaten on both sides with carpet beaters or heavy sticks until the clouds of dust which rose when they started to beat had all disappeared. Doors, windows and woodwork were all washed and the floors scrubbed before everything was put back in place and the house resumed it's normal routine.

Bungay races had been run as a two day meeting under National Hunt rules for about fifty years and was probably the biggest event of the year for the town's residents and affected them all in one way or another. These took place in April or May but preparations were being made a long time before that on and off the common. The two grandstands were opened up and running repairs carried out while the iron railings which surrounded them for the rest of the year were removed and put on one side in piles ready to erect again after the meeting and the ring where the horses were paraded was railed off to the rear of the stands. The course was about two miles long and the grass had to be cut, the potholes filled and where necessary the ground levelled between the jumps which also had to be built. The biggest of these was the water jump situated immediately in front of the stands.

These two days created employment in all sorts of ways. Many of the horses travelled in by train and arrived some time before the day of the races to be billeted all over the town particularly in the pubs where they had stables at the back for the horses and accommodation in the house for the staff to look after them. The railway goods yard was a busy place when they arrived in their special wagons for they had to be shunted from the siding they had been left in by the engine which brought them. There were no engines at Bungay and to the delight of the crowd of youngsters who gathered on the bank on the Little Common to watch, a heavy horse was used to shunt the wagons up to the goods platform so they could be unloaded. As the days of the event got nearer the number of visitors in the town increased and the hotels and inns filled up as did all other available accommodation and the whole town was caught in a wave of excitement and enthusiasm with people speaking of little else as they passed the latest information they had got from one to another about the form and chances of various horses.

On the day crowds seemed to appear from nowhere, in fact it was a well known meeting and people attended from all over the country to watch some of the horses they knew and followed ridden by nationally recognised jockeys. Everyone had a flutter on the course but win or lose it was the lively atmosphere of the day which was best remembered. The noise of the crowd and shouts of the men selling race cards, the torn up betting slips scattered all over the ground and the excitement of the build up before each race with the bookies shouting to each other as the tipsters called to people to gather around so they could try and persuade them to buy an envelope containing the name of the winner of the next race. There was an extra charge to go in the stands and the ring to see the horses parade. As the time for the start of the next race got near most people dashed off to find a spot to stand where the field could be seen approaching the jumps before they finally flashed past. With horses snorting loudly from their nostrils and mud flying from thundering hoofs, the jockeys, in their multi coloured silks and hats, shouted at them and each other as they used their crops to try and urge more speed from their mounts. A few moments later as they passed the post a loud cheer or groan went up from the stands clearly indicating to everyone whether or not the favourite was the winner.

After the excitement of the races the town hardly had time to settle down before the peace and quiet was again shattered as preparations were made on Skinner's Field at the bottom of St John's Road for the May Fair. This was primarily a horse fair held every year during the first week in May and the auctions and sales went on for three days. There was always a funfair on the site which opened in the evenings with the customary tractor used to generate the electricity to light and supply the power to drive all the amusements and stalls. Of these there were plenty including the large merry-go-round which also blared out music so loud it could be heard all over the town and made it impossible to hold a conversation if you were standing anywhere near it. The dodgems, cake walk, big wheel, mat [helter skelter] and swinging boats were always there with lots of stalls like the rock stall always situated just inside the gate so the smell met you as you entered. Rock in all shapes, sizes and flavours was laid out for you to make your choice. Then there were coconut shies [it was rated manly to knock a coconut off], quoits, shooting galleries, darts, roll a penny and many more. Positioned at the back of all these were the side shows and the boxing booth. The entry price for these varied from a penny to see something like a few reptiles or the headless woman to several pence to watch ladies dancing. One who turned up to do so with only a pair of fans for cover, had her show closed down on the first night as soon as the police were made aware of what she was doing. On the left as you entered the gate backed up against the farm buildings were salesmen with all kinds of wares laid out on a large sheet the ground. These were real professionals and their banter soon had a small crowd gathered to see what they had to offer. Nothing was sold in a straightforward way, they would pick up an article and quote what the price was then quickly say they didn't want that much, nor half as much, in fact they would let it go for a few pence. After a bit more banter if they had no takers they just talked on and then offered five razor blades, or something like that, free with every one of these articles purchased. People did buy from them and most believed they had a bargain and couldn't understand how these men were able to make a profit but they obviously did as they returned every year and many, especially the children, looked on them as part of the entertainment. These salesmen must have had an official name but they were always referred to as 'Cheap Jacks'.

Other men walked among the stalls selling small toys, fancy cardboard hats and balls made from bright coloured material, filled with sawdust and attached to a length of elastic so you could throw it at someone and retrieve it without having to go after it. Unfortunately it didn't take many throws before the elastic broke and the ball was lost. People all enjoyed the fair and there was something for everyone to spend their money on but nearly all of them made sure they held back at least a penny for a bag of chips from the stall which always stood on the road just outside the gate for no chips ever tasted like them and it would take a very strong will to walk straight past when their warm smell hit your nostrils and you could hear them sizzling in the pan.

Each morning the sales and auctions took place and the Grammar School which was situated opposite gave all the pupils a holiday for the three days the fair was on. This was just as well for at this time St John's Road could be quite dangerous as many of the men buying horses and carts wanted to try them out before handing over the money and this road was where most of the trials were done. Added to this the pubs were open all day while the fair was in town, something the visitors took full advantage of so some might well have been in high spirits when putting their new acquisitions through their paces.

Whit Monday was another Bank Holiday when everyone hoped for a fine warm day so the whole family could get out and enjoy it together. It was a lovely time of the year to be in the country where everything was green and growing fast with the air clear of dust and pollen and no flies or insects to cause annoyance and irritation. Men with gardens and allotments found this a busy time as they hurried to finish off their planting and keep the weeds under control by hoeing between the rows of seedlings and young plants. At the same time they had to try to think of new ways to outwit the birds and mice and sometimes even rabbits who were always after tasty young plants or newly planted seeds.

The time for haymaking soon arrived and everybody prayed for fine weather. It needed to be dry before it was raked up and carted to be stored or stacked for if it was damp when stacked, there was a good chance it would heat up inside and spontaneous combustion would cause it to smoulder and finally burst into flame. The farmers had their own men, horses and equipment to take care of their fields but there were a number of smallholders who had none of these and had to call on the help of the hay merchant who would arrange everything, cutting, stacking and thatching the stack to keep the rain off. Volunteers were often called in to help with the loading and unloading which was all done by passing the hay from one to another with pitch forks. The mild beer which was part of their payment could be seen in earthenware jars, cased in wicker baskets to keep it cool, swinging on the back of the hay wagon where it was hung within easy reach of the men when they got thirsty. When the weather was fine many of the children joined in and lent a hand. The actual building of the stack, which had to be put onto a base of faggots to allow air underneath, was done by the hay merchant himself as this was a skilful job and he would be called back later to cut trusses from the stack as and when they were required.

As the Summer progressed the green fields gradually turned to brown as the corn ripened ready for harvesting and the changing colours of the fruit on the trees and bushes showed it was ready to be picked. Families had their own favourite places where they could find sloes and elderberries for their home made wine and blackberries which were good to eat as they were picked and tasted even better when they were baked with apples in a pie. If there were a lot they could always be made into jam with or without the apple. After the strawberries in June there was an abundance of fresh fruit and vegetables available from the gardens and allotments and as much of it could not be stored it was passed to friends and neighbours or exchanged with another gardener for something he hadn't grown himself.

Potatoes and carrots were kept for future use by putting them in a hole lined with straw and covering them with more straw before throwing a thick layer of soil on the top ensuring a small bundle of the straw  protruded out of the top to form a kind of chimney so air could get down to them. Some fruits were bottled or dried to preserve them while onions and other vegetables were pickled in vinegar which could be bought by the pint from any public house if you took your own jug or bottle. Families who kept back yard hens and found they had more eggs than they needed when they were all laying had the choice of selling the surplus to friends or submerging them in a pail of glass water where they remained fresh enough to be used when the hens went off the lay. Eggs were much cheaper to buy at this time of the year and some people who did not keep chickens and could afford to, bought a few extra each week and stored them in this way.

Harvest time meant hard work and long hours for the farmers but many people, including the youngsters, enjoyed it. This time of the year was the easiest for the poorer classes when the weather was warm, fruit and vegetables plentiful and in the fields there was always the chance of a rabbit which could be prepared in a variety of ways to provide a nourishing meal for the family. Extra hands were needed in the fields for it was necessary to get the harvest in quickly before it got wet. Men had to use scythes to cut a road through the corn all around the outside of the field to make room for the horse pulling the binder. The binder then worked round and round in decreasing circles, leaving a trail of sheaves to be gathered by people following behind the machine. They were stood in stooks, bundles of four or five sheaves leaning against each other. When the last patch of corn in the centre was cut and all the rabbits had run the gauntlet, a wagon was brought in and moved round the field for the sheaves to be thrown up and stacked by pitch forks until they were piled as high as they could go. Then they were carted off towards the farm to be unloaded onto the threshing machine which, driven by a long slack belt attached to a very noisy tractor, separated the corn from the straw. The whole operation was a dirty and uncomfortable one for the workers. They suffered scratches from the sharp ends of straw which found it's way down the back of their necks and inside their shirts as they handled the sheaves with their pitch forks. Near the threshing machine, they worked in a constant cloud of dust which they breathed in and which stuck to their sweating bodies.

It was a time for rejoicing when the harvest was in. All the churches held their own harvest festival when the congregation contributed samples of their produce which was expertly positioned to decorate the church for the thanksgiving service. Corn dollies were everywhere with all kinds of fruit and vegetables as well as eggs and flowers. After the service these were given to local hospitals. On completion of a bumper harvest it was not unusual for a farmer to lay on a meal for his workers and their families to show his appreciation. There were several men employed on some of the farms and sometimes the only building to hold such a number was the barn. Tables and benches were set up and as dusk fell hurricane lamps were hung around them. Their dim light adding to the warm, happy atmosphere. Unfortunately not all farmers were that charitable.

August Bank Holiday was another day off for the workers and it's passing signalled the end of the Summer. The days were getting shorter and within a week or two the weather could be expected to turn colder so this was the last chance for organisations to hold their carnivals and fetes outside. The chill in the air soon called a halt to the older folk enjoying the evenings sitting outside their front doors watching the children at play and people going by. They were obliged to move inside and settle for what could be seen gazing through net curtains before the evenings pulled right in and it was too dark to see anything.

Long before November 5th. children made their effigies of Guy Fawkes and wheeled them into town on barrows or old prams clearly displaying a card which read 'A penny for the guy'. They positioned themselves in a closed doorway or on the pavement against a wall where there were lots of people passing by who might throw them a copper or two. Several shops sold fireworks but the children had to have an adult or older boy or girl to accompany them when they went to buy them as it was illegal for them to be sold to children under age. Nevertheless, youngsters with the money who wanted them usually managed to find a way to get them.

On the night, families got together round a bonfire in the back garden or on one of their allotments. Many shared a fire and pooled their fireworks for these were quite expensive when people wanted something spectacular and pretty to watch and not just penny squibs which fizzed and went off with a loud bang. It was quite a common occurrence for a child with a sparkler or someone trying to read the instructions with a lighted match to drop it into the box containing all those they still had to let off which resulted in the whole lot going up in a blaze of coloured sparks and smoke.

Rockets, catherine wheels and various fountains seemed the most popular except among the teenagers who preferred squibs and jumping jacks they could let off behind unsuspecting people as they went around the town in small groups. They knew they were not allowed to carry or let off fireworks in the streets and the police would confiscate them if they were caught. Most carried one or two in each pocket with the rest tucked in their belt under their shirt or in their socks under their trousers but even so the local bobby was fully aware of all the tricks and had no trouble finding them. Everyone was warned repeatedly of the dangers if the instructions given on every box and individual firework were not strictly followed but there were those who ignored such advice as they went in search of excitement goading each other on to throw a squib or banger into a front garden or doorway as they ran off. Knowing they might bump into the local policeman and have to run for it only added to their exhilaration. Fortunately the accidents which occurred were usually self inflicted minor burns and the youngsters high spirits rarely caused any lasting damage. One or two of the wilder ones were caught from time to time by older members of the community who generally favoured the idea of administering any punishment they considered appropriate on the spot.

Armistice Day on November 11th. was observed by everyone and a penny or two was readily put into a collection tin for a poppy. Even the very young, who had little idea what it was really all about were aware of how solemn an occasion it was. At eleven o'clock in the morning the printing works hooter sounded and was the signal for everything to stop for the two minutes silence, traffic in the streets came to a halt and no matter where people were, in shops, at work or in the home they stood in silence and remembered those who had not returned from the war.

The remembrance service was held at St Mary's Church on the following Sunday when every seat would be taken and those that couldn't get in clustered round the door outside. Leading up to the service, both young and old members of almost every organisation formed a parade and headed by a band they marched through the town with the men who had served in all branches of the services proudly displaying their medals and carrying the British Legion Banner. They halted opposite the memorial bearing the names of all those that died and representatives placed their wreaths and poppies around it. This was a very emotional time for many especially during the service when the roll of honour was read. A trumpeter then sounded the last post and two minutes silence, for everyone to meditate personally on those loved ones who had suffered and gave their lives followed. The trumpeter then sounded the carry on. Fifteen or sixteen years had done little to relieve some men and women of the shock and trauma caused by the war and there were very few who were not affected in some way by the loss or injury of relatives and friends.

Days were short now and nights getting longer as the winter set in but there was Christmas to look forward to and it was not long before the shops made it obvious it was on the way as one by one they put up trimmings and decorated their windows. Their clubs had been running for several months and now was the time those that had been fortunate enough to be able to save a few shillings could decide what they wanted to spend it on and place their order. No matter how poor families were they all made every effort to ensure there was a special dinner on Christmas Day and a little something extra for the children to find in their stockings. To ensure this they had to put away the odd tin of fruit or perhaps a tin of salmon or anything they could afford all through the year to keep until this time arrived.

Children who had been quickly out with their guy before Guy Fawkes now, with a candle in a jam jar to light their way, turned their attention to carol singing. Usually not more than three or four of them together went from door to door and rendered a verse or two of a well known carol or at least as much of it as they could, for very often they didn't know all of the words, then knocked on the door for their reward. Some started too early and were told to come back in a few days, others tried to get away with singing only a few lines and were politely told 'not tonight thank you', most gave value for money and in the week leading up to Christmas people looked forward to hearing them and gave them a copper or two, some even invited them in for a hot drink and a cake. Unfortunately it was spoilt by those who told their friends which houses they had called at and got a good reception so generous householders often got a constant flow of children knocking at their door all evening.

The Salvation Army, as well as some other choirs, went round the streets in the town accompanied by their band rendering their carols at various places where they attracted small clusters of

159

people who stopped to listen and put money in their collection for charity while other members took their boxes from door to door. It was not unusual for some members of the public to join in the singing

All the families who were able to had a Christmas tree indoors which was trimmed to size and stood up in a bucket or large flower pot then lit by small fancy candles in metal holders clipped onto the branches. Many of the trimmings were made by the children at school or at home by pasting coloured strips to form a chain or using sheets of crepe paper cut up into various shapes and sizes to make decorations to go round the pictures or on the tree. Small empty packets and boxes would be covered in coloured wrappers or silver paper, tied with ribbon or wool and put on the tree to look like presents while small trinkets and toys were wrapped carefully to be given to each other on Christmas Day. Holly could be bought at the shops but lots of people knew where to find it in the countryside and this was placed above the pictures on the walls and the mirror which always hung over the mantlepiece or pinned, like the mistletoe, above the doors. Trimmings were all held up with drawing pins which held very well in the plaster on the walls and ceilings of the older houses but were sometimes a problem to take out and when a knife was used a lump of plaster often fell out with it.

There were greetings cards for the children to design and colour with their crayons and paints to give to friends. Parents, who could afford to, exchanged cards but usually only with people close to them and any they received were placed around the room on the mantlepiece, sideboard and piano [if there was one], to compliment the decorations. If the house was large enough to have a front room this was one time it was always used and a fire would be lit a few days before Christmas to make sure it was thoroughly aired before the family moved in to trim up. This was a busy time for the women. Not only were they involved in all the preparations of getting presents etc. which they did with the other members of the family but they had all the groceries and food to order and get in, as well as the baking to do a day before as everyone looked forward to their mince pies and sausage rolls and then there was dinner to cook on Christmas Day. The cake was made, iced and decorated some time earlier as were the puddings which all the family took turns to stir and make a wish. A few silver threepenny pieces would be put into these after mixing which encouraged the children to eat some in the hope they would find one in their helping.

This was a happy time for most people but much more so for the families of the better off who had a round of parties to attend before Christmas where they had crackers and balloons and a table laden with such things as jellies, blanc manges, trifles, ham, potted meat and cucumber sandwiches, sponges, cakes, biscuits and of course a chocolate log. Games were supervised by parents and varied according to the ages of the children from 'Ring a Roses' and 'The Bells of St Lemon's' for the very young to something like 'Postman's Knock' or 'Sardines' for the older ones. There were a number of professional and amateur entertainers locally who were sometimes called in to amuse the children with their puppet shows or conjuring tricks and these were well received by those who were able to afford them.

For a large number of people Christmas was not like that. It was just a time for the family to get together to celebrate and their festivities only lasted the two days, just Christmas and Boxing Day. It did mean in many cases that grandparents, parents and brothers and sisters all got together to pool their resources and spend the two days at one house which was great for the children and even better for the mother who might now get some help with the cooking and washing up.

Children of all ages went to bed early on Christmas Eve no matter if they believed in Santa Claus or not and they all hung up a stocking or, in the case of the better off, a pillow case knowing when they awoke there would be something in it. All found it difficult to get to sleep and many wanted to stay awake to see who filled the stocking but they would eventually drop off. In the larger houses the traditional glass of port wine and mince pie was put on the table for Santa before the children went up and father did not find it difficult to remember to dispose of them before he retired for the night. Long before the first rays of daylight children were opening their presents, some found everything they wanted but others were disappointed. Many found their stocking hanging on the bedpost with a few nuts in the toe and filled with an apple, an orange and other fruit and sweets, a colouring book and box of wax crayons, a ball, some plasticine and other simple toys like beads and marbles or even a bow and arrows for the boys and a rag doll for the girls. Whatever it was they were excited and happy to receive. As they got older, youngsters all enjoyed books of nursery rhymes which they soon learned off by heart and these were always popular until they gave way to annuals and the more well known children's books. Households who had a large tree sometimes had their presents laid out underneath it and in the morning when they got up the whole family sat round and watched as each was handed their parcels to open.

At various times through the year the town was visited by fairs and the circus which were sited on the Little Common. Their coming was announced by the numerous bills which appeared overnight on posts and billboards. The fairs were like small editions of the May Fair but there were plenty of rides and stalls and side shows. Each show had it's own small tent, on the outskirts along the top of the railway bank. There you could have your fortune told, see the tattooed lady or perhaps box a few rounds for which you might get paid a bob or two if you happened to win. The rock stall was invariably just inside the gate so the familiar smell of that and the tractor together with the noise and music met you and gave a tingle of excitement as you passed through. Outside the gate the chip stall was set up ready to serve those who had saved the money for their pennyworth of chips when it was time to go home.

The circus was a family business where everyone had to help with everything and when they changed their venue the horses, elephants and other larger animals were walked between towns. This was much to the delight of the residents of the houses they passed but not to the road sweeper who had to clear up after them. The ring inside the tent was quite small and the seats were no more than planks of wood raised one above the other so you sat on one and put your feet on the one below where someone else was sitting. They were most uncomfortable and quite dangerous as small children could easily slip through the gap between them. Lions in a cage, bears, elephants, seals as well as horses and a host of other animals visited the Little Common from time to time accompanied by the traditional clowns and artists showing their skills on all kinds of things like the trapeze and tight-rope, In many instances it was the same performers doing different acts. When it was over, for two or three pence, you could visit the animals at the back and watch them being fed.

During this decade the people celebrated two major occasions with the rest of the country, the Silver Jubilee of King George V in 1935 and the Coronation of King George V1 in 1937. The sun shone and a beautiful day dawned for the Jubilee, everyone in the town was caught up in the excitement and wanted to do their bit to express their loyalty and affection for a King who had worked hard to get closer to his subjects. He started to broadcast his Christmas Day message to the Commonwealth in 1932 and it was unfortunate there were not more people with access to a wireless able to listen to it although those attending the cinema at a later date would hear extracts in the Pathé Gazette news. A national holiday was declared to celebrate the Jubilee and everyone had time to organise a day to remember. The streets and roads were all decorated with flags and bunting and there was hardly a house in the town without a flag or something colourful hanging from the windows.

The Common was the venue for the festivities and one of the main events was a football match played in fancy dress on the pitch in front of the golf house to the great amusement of all the spectators. The costumes were very good and the antics hilarious especially Will Hay who played on the wing and carried a carpet beater which was used to good effect to break down the opposing defenders. There were organised races, running, egg and spoon and sack race etc. for young and old. Towards the top of the first hill were two greasy poles, one vertical where the first man to reach the top won a pig and the other horizontal where two people starting opposite ends and sitting astride it moved to the centre and tried to dislodge each other by aiming and swinging a bag of straw, which they grasped in one hand, without falling off. There was so much grease on the vertical pole that hardly anyone climbed more than a few feet before slowly sliding to the bottom covered in a sticky mess but it was all great fun for those looking on.

The larger of the grandstands was opened and all the children under fifteen who lived in the town filed into it and sat down to receive a commemorative mug, which was duly filled with lemonade and a bag meal which contained something like a bread roll with cheese, a cake, an apple and a packet of crisps. A dance was organised for the adults to round off a highly successful day which finished with everyone very tired but exhilarated.

For a brief period after the death of George V, Edward V111 who was next in line became King. As Prince of Wales he had been quite popular with the public but the scandal of his affair with a divorced woman reached even the most remote areas and jokes were freely related and repeated everywhere from the local pubs to the school playgrounds. They were short lived however for in December 1936 even before his coronation he abdicated and George V1 ascended the throne. Production of souvenirs was already well in hand and had to be stopped and changed to depict the new monarch.

Celebrations to mark the Coronation of George V1 were planned to equal those of the Jubilee. The inhabitants again decorated the town with flags and bunting and looked forward to the day with eager anticipation. When it arrived, the dawn broke to reveal dark clouds with steady rain which continued to fall until well into the afternoon completely washing out all the carefully prepared programme. Arrangements were quickly made for the children to muster at the Council School in Wingfield Street to receive their Coronation mug and bag meal and then make their way to the

New Theatre where they were entertained with suitable cartoons and a film. When they came out the rain had stopped but it was too late and much too wet for any outdoor festivities. The dance which was arranged for the evening went ahead as planned and was well supported but nothing could be said or done to hide the disappointment felt by all who had worked so hard for many weeks to ensure this would be another spectacular day to remember.

UPPER OLLAND STREET - THE JUBILEE DECORATIONS

# CHAPTER 13.

## HEALTH AND WELFARE.

Employers had two stamps to buy every week for each person working for them, one to be stuck on their unemployment card and the other on their national insurance card. Six months unbroken contributions entitled the employee to benefit if they were out of work or sick but only for a limited time and the benefits were small. Anyone having their employment terminated was given their cards and had to attend the labour exchange where they signed on for benefit. They then had to present themselves and sign three days a week to prove they were not working and they were looking for a job. Self employed people or those not working and not on the dole could buy the stamps from the post office if they wished to keep their cards up to date, for everyone had to fill a certain number of national insurance cards before they were entitled to a pension when they retired at the age of sixty five.

There were two general medical practices in the town each consisting of a doctor with a partner, one situated in Trinity Street and the other in Lower Olland Street. Doctors were very highly respected by everyone in the town and generally, although there was no real reason why they should be, most of the younger generation were fearful of them even though some made every effort to allay this. Perhaps the customary long wait in the waiting room where nobody dared to speak louder than a whisper did much to increase any tension they might already be feeling. Other than weekends and bank holidays the surgery was open in the mornings and evenings. People wishing to see the doctor reported to the dispenser, who also acted as receptionist, then sat down quietly in the waiting room where there were magazines to read although none were likely to have been published within the previous three or four years.

When it was their turn to go in, the dispenser handed them their medical records which they took with them and handed to the doctor. There was usually a very long wait of anything up to a couple of hours and after consultation patients requiring medicine went back to the dispenser and waited while he mixed it up for them. If it was a prescription he did not have he would send out for it then place it, clearly labelled, on a table in the surgery for someone to return and collect at a pre-arranged time. Most medicines were issued in a special flat bottle which was moulded with the doses marked in the glass on the back and a flat panel for the label on the front while pills were given out in small round flat boxes. The doctors spent a great deal of their time doing house calls and many sick people, particularly children, were confined to their beds in their own homes. In fact that seemed to be the first move made on anyone who was found to have a high temperature which meant the doctor then had to return daily to check to see if it had gone down.

Every year the doctors were kept busy as the usual epidemics of children's complaints spread through the schools. Every child was expected to have measles, chicken pox and mumps at some time and these were treated, like most other children's illnesses, in their own home. Throat infections were a problem among youngsters and there was a constant flow of children going into hospital for a few days to have their tonsils removed. This caused them quite a lot of pain and discomfort at the time but looking back at their short stay in hospital the clearest memory for many was the jelly and ice cream they were fed afterwards.

Before consulting the doctor many people tried treating minor illnesses with old fashioned remedies that had been handed down from mother to daughter and great faith was put in ointments and oils which could be rubbed into aching and painful joints and muscles. Children who suffered with coughs and breathing ailments had their chests rubbed regularly every night with something like Vick and during the day, to keep the cold out, they would have a large square of Thermogene fixed inside the front of their vest with safety pins. Each time the vest was taken off or put on the Thermogene dragged across the face so the dusty content was breathed up the nose, irritating it and often causing a fit of sneezing.

Lots of cures were passed on for things like chilblains, corns and warts and no doubt they worked for some as did the bread poultice for toothache and other swellings but usually temporary relief was the most that could be expected from such treatment. Aspros were the most widely used pain killers and were available in large and small boxes or in a strip of just five tablets for a couple of pence at all sorts of shops and were used mainly for the relief of headaches and other women's complaints. Some parents made sure their children were kept regular by giving them a weekly dose of syrup of figs or for the more stubborn, senapods, while they themselves never missed taking their Beecham's pill at the weekend. Some of the less robust children had a daily spoonful of cod liver oil and malt to help ward off ills during the cold weather.

Any time a child had a complaint which seemed serious the doctor was sent for and any case or even suspected case of something like scarlet fever was treated with grave concern and the patient immediately taken to hospital and put into an isolation ward. There were cases of rickets and complaints resulting from malnutrition among the poorer families but these were not nearly as prevalent in the country as they were in the large towns and cities. Quite a lot of young people suffered from appendicitis and were rushed off to hospital to have their appendix removed. This was quite serious and resulted in a number of deaths. Nobody seemed to know exactly what caused it and it was generally believed that something swallowed found it's way into the appendix and got stuck there. One of the things it was thought might be responsible were the small chips always visibly missing from the enamel dishes which everyone used when baking pies or rice puddings. True or not, as a consequence many people refused to eat food which was cooked in them. Lots of the aches and twinges complained of by youngsters were dismissed by their parents as 'growing pains' although very few of them had any idea what these were.

Adults, particularly the working class, did not generally consult the doctor unless they were seriously ill, thought they had something contagious or were in pain. Generally they treated their ailments themselves as best they could. Cancer was a common cause of death and there was very little treatment available, all that could be done was to ease the pain as much as possible. Several local residents were known to be suffering from tuberculosis. This could be seen and easily confirmed when they were out and had a coughing fit and were obliged to spit blood in the gutter. It was believed that this disease, commonly known as consumption, was largely contracted through milk supplies and legislation was brought in to have all herds tested. This actually meant the bulls had to be tested every six months which was not very satisfactory as it could be infected a month after the test and then spread the disease for five months before it was detected. This disease mostly affected people's lungs and there seemed to be no guaranteed cure. Some sufferers who could afford to had an outhouse built in the garden where they were able to maximise their intake of fresh air and were less likely to pass the infection on to other members of their family.

The most prevalent complaint among the upper and middle classes was stomach ulcers, believed to be caused by tension and worry and well publicised by the Hollywood films who always seemed to have their top executives and tycoons reaching for a bottle of pills as soon as they were put under any kind of pressure. At a certain level having an ulcer seemed to be almost an essential qualification for some appointments. However, it could be a very serious situation for those that did suffer with them. Many people in the town were employed on the land and whenever they cut or injured themselves, no matter how slightly, Tetanus was something they always feared. Known as 'lock jaw' because of the very painful spasms in the muscles, particularly in the jaw, this was caused by bacteria, found in the soil in this part of the country, getting into a wound. A less serious complaint common among adults was Quinsy which affected their tonsils and might have been conducive to the numerous cases of tonsilitus found among the children.

District nurses played a big part in the health and welfare of ordinary people and were heavily relied upon by many families. Their only means of transport was a bicycle with a basket fixed to the front handlebars to carry their bag. As soon as a woman had confirmed she was pregnant she contacted the nurse and booked her for the birth as all babies, unless there were complications, were born in their own homes. Arrangements were made well in advance for someone, a relation, neighbour or sometimes just a friend, to look after both mother and child as well as any other children she might already have. After the birth, no matter how well the mother seemed, she had to stay in bed for at least a week and was not allowed off the bed for the first three days. Needless to say many broke these rules especially when they had other very young children. They usually did so when there was no chance of being caught by the nurse for these women were devoted to their work and although they performed their tasks with tenderness and understanding they were very serious disciplinarians. If the father was working he could not cope without help for he would never be given time off for such an event and even if he had been it is unlikely he could afford to lose any wages at a time when financial demands on him were increasing. When the time arrived someone was sent to get the nurse who delivered the baby herself and only had a doctor present if she thought it necessary for some reason or the mother specifically asked for one.

The midwife's skill was never in doubt. How could it be when Nurse Britten, the resident nurse in Bungay delivered hundreds of babies and her career spanned sufficient years for her to deliver the babies of mothers who had also been delivered by her? These things often happened in the night and if the father was at home when the nurse arrived she immediately instructed him to light the copper and have as much hot water available as possible. This not only fulfiled a need but kept his mind off what was going on. After it was all over he had to advise all interested parties and probably wet the babies head with his friends down at the pub. He also had to register the birth at the Registry Office in Upper Olland Street and contact the local clergyman to arrange for his wife to be churched. No mother went out anywhere after giving birth until she had been officially blessed in church.The christening would be organised at a later date.

Older people also put demands on the nurse especially when they were bedridden. Families generally took on the responsibility of caring for the older generation and parents, finding themselves on their own when one partner died, often moved in to live with and be looked after by their children. Alternatively if it was a large family they might all rally round to look after them in their own home until they were no longer able to do anything for themselves. Then one, usually the oldest daughter, would take them in and care for them. The nurse was always available to pop in and administer any medical attention and give any advice they might need.

Only very serious cases were sent to hospital and they were usually emergencies. Minor operations were carried out by the local doctors at All Hallows Hospital at Ditchingham which was run by the nuns from the adjoining nunnery while the more serious cases went to the Norfolk and Norwich Hospital. This could be quite a shock to many people who had never been subjected to strict discipline for there were rules and regulations which had to be adhered to no matter what your circumstances. Beds were in straight rows down both sides of the wards with exactly the same distance between them. These were moved when the wards were cleaned and the floors polished by trainee and junior nurses then carefully put back into position.

Before going off duty the night staff worked their way down the ward making the beds and turning the top sheet back neatly and without creases and from that time they had to remain like that with nothing on them, particularly not newspapers and no one was ever permitted to sit on them. When the matron did her rounds each morning everything had to be clean and tidy and everyone quiet and still. The day started with all patients being awakened at about five o'clock to wash or be washed which meant it was a very long day.

Visitors were allowed for two hours in the afternoon and then again in the evening but many people were unable to get away or afford the fares to visit more than once or twice a week. The hospitals did an excellent job but they were not very nice places to be in for as well as being subjected to unfamiliar discipline the food was plain and rather basic and the time passed very slowly.

Everyone was becoming aware of the importance of looking after their teeth, particularly the children who were told repeatedly by their parents that all their teeth would rot if they ate too many sweets. Later in the decade some councils arranged for dentists to call at their schools and examine the pupils teeth and if they needed treatment a letter was sent to their parents for permission to proceed with it. Unfortunately dental treatment was quite expensive and not many ordinary folk could afford to have regular check ups. Even if they could there was a big deterrent in the fact that it was very painful and most people waited until their toothache was unbearable and every known home cure had been tried before they consulted the dentist. By this time their cheek might be blown up and very red and there would be a large gumboil underneath the affected tooth. Before pulling the tooth the dentist injected it and the patient returned to the waiting room for fifteen minutes while the whole side of his face as well as his tongue, lips and nose went numb. Returning to the chair it took only a moment or two to have the tooth pulled out, to rinse the mouth and pay the two shillings and sixpence which was the usual charge for one extraction. There were two dentists in the town and many tales about their expertise abounded, none of which gave any encouragement to anyone requiring attention. Fillings were always painful and although one dentist retained a drill operated with a treadle like those used on sewing machines, he had progressed and now used a new electric one. The problem with that was, as he drilled the head became hot and felt as though he was drilling through the gum, then when he stopped to see if he had taken enough out or to change the drill head he used an air jet to clean out the loose pieces and this seemed to hit the nerve as though it was a red hot needle. Nothing was done to numb the tooth before this work was done but cotton wool was packed all around it to keep it dry and a pipe, usually held in place by the patient, hung over the bottom lip to suck up the saliva as it came into the mouth. Anyone who could not stand the thought of the needle for the injection when a tooth had to be pulled could, if they wished, be anaesthetised with gas which was the usual method used on people who required a large number of their teeth to be taken out at the same time. Perhaps the worst part of attending the dentist was sitting in the waiting room awaiting your turn and pretending to read an out of date magazine while looking at the faces of others around you and praying they would be called in before you.

# CHAPTER 14.

## A SUMMARY.

Everyone was affected in some way by the rapid changes that took place during this decade. The installation of electricity into homes not only improved people's standard of living but put them in touch with the rest of the world and consequently raised their expectations. This was happening at a time when the motor was taking over everywhere and travel became a reality and not just a dream. The changes accelerated in 1938 when the country prepared for war and unemployment and lack of money was no longer people's main worry. If anything was needed to convince people of the seriousness of the situation it was when the whole population of the town were summoned in alphabetical order, at various times, to the courthouse to be fitted and supplied with a gas mask.

Attitudes changed and social barriers came down as members of all classes got together to do whatever they were called on to do to assist in the defence of the country. People accepted these changes as a necessity and only looked forward to the end of hostilities when, with families again united, they could plan for the future. In the meantime they took each day as it came ever fearful of the future but determined in their efforts to all pull together to save their country.

Life became quite hectic for everyone and there was no longer any spare time to be idly passed away. As the younger men, starting with the eighteen year olds, were progressively called to arms the older generation were enrolled for various duties after they finished their days work with the ARP, LDV, police, fire brigade or any of the many back up services who all needed more people. Factories, businesses and schools etc. organised their own firewatchers who worked on a roster to ensure there was always someone on duty through the night. It was inevitable this would bring together and form bonds between all kinds of men from different walks of life just as the armed forces did. Under different circumstances they would never have given each other so much as a nod if they passed in the street.

The women too had services to support and while many gave up their home life to do so, others of all ages who stayed at home gave up their time to help in a multitude of ways from organising and running canteens for the forces to knitting balaclavas or collecting old silk stockings for sailors to wear under their socks in their sea boots to keep their feet warm. No matter what their age or ability there was a job for everyone and never before had the population been bound by such strong fellowship.

With the whole town caught up in these frenzied activities it is unlikely anyone ever looked back to see what was being lost as they quickly learned to take for granted the newly acquired benefits they now all enjoyed. The changes in their social standards over a few years had been quite dramatic and it was now difficult to understand how people living under the conditions that existed in the early 1930's found anything to inspire them to persevere. However they had never had much comfort or experienced the pleasures which modern services made possible and it was unlikely they ever contemplated such things until they were brought to their attention by the cinema and radio. It would have been easy for anyone to remind themselves of the conditions they had left behind as many surrounding villages were still without electricity and piped water and even more awaited flush toilets and sewerage. There was one popular saying which was often repeated throughout the decade, 'what you have never had you never miss'.

One thing that came with this progress almost unnoticed was noise. In a small market town much of the tranquillity of the countryside disappeared and with it went some of the patience and serenity which had been one of the people's biggest strengths earlier in the decade. Many familiar sounds were no longer noticed and those that were could not be as easily detected for without a clear sound to attract attention sightings of some of the countryside's biggest attractions were missed. Everyone had been aware of the sound of the trains running into the station because it was the only sound breaking the silence at the time, as was the noise made by the wings of swans or geese as they flew overhead and the house sparrows nesting under the tiles who had everyone awake early in the morning. There were several rookeries in the town including those in St Mary's School grounds, alongside Trinity Church and at the doctor's surgery in Lower Olland Street and everyone living in the vicinity was made well aware of them by the noise the birds made when they were nesting. Swallows and swifts were to be seen in great numbers especially when they were preparing to migrate and congregated on the telegraph wires. Although the swallows and house martins made a lot of mess wherever they built their nests, householders hoped they would  come back next year for it was said they always returned to a happy home. On a Winters afternoon, just before darkness closed in, flocks of noisy crows let everybody know the day was ending as they flew over on their way home or as children often commented, 'they're going home from school'.

It was the distinctness of familiar sounds that was most missed, like the blacksmith at work on his anvil, the clang of trucks being shunted at the goods yard, the town clock striking, the clip-clop of horses hoofs on the road, a cycle bell ringing, a child shouting, a dog barking in the distance or any one of a thousand other common noises which broke the silence. The very thought of some of these noises immediately conjures up a picture in the mind which not only brings back memories of places and events but also revives strong feelings of tranquillity

On Winter evenings when the children were in bed, wooden armchairs were pulled up to the open fire which made a quiet roar and crackle as the flames leaped up and helped to light the room as they reflected dancing shadows on the walls. There wasn't much to talk about and this was the time for the housewife to knit or sew and catch up on all the odd jobs she hadn't had time to do during the day while her husband rested and puffed at his pipe or cigarette while he stared thoughtfully into the fire. The only other noise would be the ticking of the clock, unless the weather was bad, when the wind whistling through the draughty doors or the rain beating on the window broke the silence.

On a Summer evening the doors and windows would be wide open and folk might step outside to converse with their neighbours while the children played nearby. Some even carried out a chair and sat by the door watching and greeting people as they passed by. The town clock reminded them of the time every fifteen minutes and the odd horse and cart rumbled by with the horse's hoofs clip-clopping on the hard road as it went on it's way but there was little else to disturb the peace and quiet of the surroundings.

Times best remembered were the warm days when the gorse on the common was in bloom and the countryside was green and lush. Sunday afternoon walks in any direction out of the town revealed wild life in abundance from the deer roaming wild and free on the large estates down to the smallest field mouse and insects. Nothing was more relaxing than a stroll by the river where the swans glided gracefully against a slow moving stream and the silence was only broken by a skylark as it took to the air or the cry of a water hen frightened by a movement in the water, perhaps a rat was after it's eggs or chicks. Even the slightest breeze rustled the leaves in the trees and the only unnatural sound might be the splash of oars and the rippling of water against the bow as a rowing boat moved gently upstream or when the wind was in the right direction, the sound of a train pulling out of the station or whistling as it approached the level crossings.

Being brought up in the country everyone learned to have respect for it at an early age and as they walked around they took for granted what people are now taught as the country code. They may not always have kept to the footpaths round the fields when they were after blackberries and they might have taken the odd turnip or swede but then there was only ever one or two locals at any one time so any damage or loss to the farmer was minimal. Nevertheless some farmers objected to anyone going on their fields and these were probably the ones who attracted youngsters most when they were looking for a bit of excitement. There was not much danger of leaving a gate open because where there were footpaths they had stiles to climb over or a kissing gate which was a gate that swung in a U-shaped frame so only one person was able to pass through in one direction at a time and there was no chance of an animal larger than a dog being able to get through.

At the beginning of the decade the pace of life was still very much regulated by the simple basic way people had to live and most of their time was taken up just feeding and clothing their families and keeping a roof of sorts over their heads. Those working on the land had much of their work load governed by the seasons and of course, the fact they worked with animals with whom a strict routine had to be adhered to if the best was to be got from them. If there was a poor harvest, which was invariably the result of bad weather, everyone suffered in one way or another and during adverse weather conditions they could often only wait patiently for an improvement before being able to get on with their tasks, for they had no way of making things happen outside their usual routine, there was a correct way to do things and a right time and that is how they had to be done.

Buses travelling to and from Norwich towards the end of the week sometimes found the road blocked by a flock of sheep or a herd of cattle being driven on foot to market and were delayed while the drovers, sometimes assisted by a dog, moved them to one side to make room for any traffic to pass. The number of people owning cars was on the increase but they were very expensive and still not completely reliable. The woodwork master at the Grammar School travelled from Beccles twice a week in his motor and it was quite a common sight after school had finished to see him being pushed down the drive by half a dozen conscripted boys as he endeavoured to get it started.

In these days nobody ever seemed to be in a hurry and yet they always managed to have everything done on time. Perhaps it was because everyone had a fairly strict routine, like the housewife who did the washing on Monday, ironed on Tuesday, baked on Thursday, bathed the family on Saturday night etc.. Without such a regulated life style the work would never have got done especially if there were several in the family. Even one child's demands of it's mother were many and there was always extra tasks to be fitted in such as cleaning the oil lamps and trimming the wicks to ensure they burned without smoking, or making the dough to give it time to rise in readiness for the next days bread. A lot of women baked their own bread two or three times a week and the dough was usually left covered in a bowl beside the fire overnight.

Conditions for all classes have continued to improve ever since the 1930's and with each passing decade ordinary people become materially better off as new labour saving devices are discovered and the hum drum chores are taken out of everyday life. Things are now taken for granted that had not even been thought of in the days referred to in this book and everyone still looks forward to see what further acquisition is required to improve their quality of life. We have now evolved too far to compare the citizens of today with those of the 1930's but if we could, it would be interesting to discover how much the material and social advantages, which are now almost an automatic right, contribute to happiness. Our parents and grandparents suffered from the same basic causes of stress and worry as the people of today, that is earning enough to support a family and keep a home together. Somehow they managed to be happier and more contented with the little they had than anyone seems to be now when everything is done to make life so much easier for them.

ST MARY'S STREET